THE
RANCHER
TAKES A WIFE

ALSO BY RICHMOND P. HOBSON, JR.

Grass Beyond the Mountains
Nothing Too Good for a Cowboy

RICHMOND P. HOBSON, JR.

THE
RANCHER
TAKES A WIFE

A TRUE ACCOUNT OF LIFE ON THE
LAST GREAT CATTLE FRONTIER

To my little daughter, Cathy

Seal Books and colophon are registered trademarks of
Random House of Canada Limited

THE RANCHER TAKES A WIFE
Seal Books/published by arrangement with
McClelland & Stewart
McClelland & Stewart edition published 1978
Seal Books edition published 2015

Library and Archives of Canada Cataloguing in Publication
data is available upon request.

ISBN: 978-1-4000-2664-7

Cover design by Five Seventeen
Cover image: © Konrad Wothe / Picture Press / Getty Images

Printed and bound in the USA

Published in Canada by Seal Books,
a division of Random House of Canada Limited

www.penguinrandomhouse.ca

10 9 8 7 6 5 4 3 2 1

Penguin
Random
House

CONTENTS

Foreword

FAR BACK IN THE INTERIOR of British Columbia, beyond the land of the Cariboo and the Chilcotin plateau, rises a vast and only partially explored wilderness slashed by deep gorges and dark mysterious mountain ranges inhabited by moose and timber wolves and giant grizzly bears.

This maze of jungles, swamps and grasslands is drained by an enormous system of creeks, streams, rivers and clear slow-flowing lakes all eventually merging to form the Nechako and the Blackwater rivers. In local Indian language Nechako means "land of the clear waters."

During the spring and summer months the grass-loaded valleys on the headwaters of these mighty rivers are like oases in the hundreds of miles of green spruce jungles that surround them. High bunch-grass hills stretch up lush and naked above transparent waters, a paradise for geese and ducks and big game, cattle and man.

But when the long frosty winter nights settle over the valleys on the headwaters of the Nechako and the Blackwater, and the mountain passes fill with snow, the country suddenly changes to a cold isolated silent range cut off from the outside world for months at a time—a frozen deserted wilderness—where disaster and death allow animal or man few mistakes.

Into this strange land beyond the beyond I had the colossal audacity to transplant my city-raised, interior-decorator bride several years ago—and this is the story of what happened.

CHAPTER I

The Bride Meets the Frontier

A MIDWINTER SLEIGH TRIP through the frozen uninhabited backlands of British Columbia's northern interior was routine business for me, for I had been manager of the Frontier Cattle Company for many years, but to land my young bride safely and happily on the remote snow-drifted Batnuni Ranch presented any number of problems.

From Gloria's comfortable home in Vancouver we were traveling some five hundred miles north by train to the little one-hundred-horse village of Vanderhoof, where we would switch from the warmth of the stateroom on the Canadian National Railway to horse-drawn sleigh and saddle horses.

From Vanderhoof we would break trail for seventy-five miles across two minor mountain ranges. This last stage of our journey would take anywhere from four to eight days, depending on snow conditions in the mountains. We would be sleeping out in the snowdrifts for several nights.

The things that worried me most were that Gloria could catch pneumonia, freeze to death, or become completely disgusted with her husband's way of life before she became acclimatized.

And so—as the train banged and rattled northward
that January in 1944, I filled Gloria in with glowing
and exaggerated descriptions of the beautiful bushland,
the sleek Hereford cattle, the smart horses, the heroic
people and my keen-brained mongrel dog that she
would soon see. The way I painted the picture it must
have sounded as if northern British Columbia were a
sort of sunny Shangri-la instead of a vast frozen solitude
with Vanderhoof one of the few man-made dots in a
rugged maze of uninhabited mountains, canyons and
swamps, larger than the states of Oregon, Washington
and California all thrown together.

We had spent the first three weeks of our married life
in the palatial comfort of the Empress Hotel in Victoria,
and in Gloria's spacious home in Vancouver, where nine
fireplaces burned cheerfully, and the contrast in sur-
roundings at five-thirty A.M. on that pitch-dark twenty-
below-zero morning, when the train groaned across the
frozen rails into Vanderhoof, must have given my bride
quite a jolt.

In the pre-dawn darkness, Vanderhoof's dimly lit
station was almost obscured in great hissing clouds of
steam rolling up from beneath the cars.

The porter, Gloria and I hurriedly gathered together
the vast assortment of Gloria's luggage, while I threw my
thirty years' gatherings into my battered, long-suffering
dunnage bag and beat-up suitcase, and we all slipped and
slid around on the ice-crusted platform.

My ranch foreman, blond, square-jawed Harold
Dwinnell, and his wife, Lucille, surged up out of the
darkness with loud exclamations of relief.

"Everything's all lined up for the newlyweds," yelled Harold over the creak and crunch of the departing train, "but that winter trail over the mountains is as cold as ever."

The train noise grew faint in the distance; silence and darkness settled down around us. A horse stomped the hard-packed snow and snorted into the frost. Lucille led Gloria towards a white-frosted team and sleigh, tied behind the station.

Harold picked up the lines, and Mike and Bud, the wheel team of a four-up, swung the outfit around, the sleigh runners biting into the snow as we glided towards a single row of lights in the distance.

"This is thrilling," Gloria called. "I know I'm going to love it all."

"I hope so," I answered dubiously, shivering in my business suit and overcoat.

Vanderhoof was like home to me. I had trailed pack trains and beef drives into the village for the past eight years. I knew practically every man, and most of the horse and dog population, of the district.

Many bets and wagers had been made as to whether Rich Hobson would actually land a real live bride here in the back country. Speculation as to what Gloria would look like, how she would fit in and how long she would last had been rife ever since articles and pictures of our wedding had appeared in the Vancouver papers. I knew only too well that a rowdy but well-meaning celebration was inevitable and an enormous amount of liquid spirits would be consumed before we slid out of the little town. At thirty-six years of age, in top range condition, I not only looked forward to the ordeal but was outrageously optimistic about the outcome.

After I had become engaged to Gloria in Vancouver, I returned to Vanderhoof to announce proudly at my bachelor party that I was going to bring back a strikingly beautiful, intelligent, young blond bride, a girl with a terrific sense of humor who understood politics, books, the world situation, men, horses and cows.

The bachelor party in Bob Reid's Frontier Hotel lasted for nearly three days, but Bob was extremely thoughtful when he handed the participants the bill which included two broken day beds, three demolished chairs, a cracked washbasin, a shattered chiffonier and a large assortment of smashed china and glassware.

Bob Reid chuckled when he reminded me of certain commitments I had made during the height of the celebration.

"Rich," he said, "if you're really preparing to marry this dream girl you're sure starting out the hard way."

I cut in on Bob. "What have I done now? We've had our stampede here at Reid's Hotel—not in Gloria's home city."

A broad grin spread across Bob's slightly red face.

"Don't you remember all the plans you made with your best man and your string of ushers? Sam Cocker, Pat Patterson, Maynard Kerr, Skookum Davidson and me— and I'm the only one that's not going. Think that one over, my boy."

A fast picture of these characters flashed across my mind. I cringed down in my chair. My mouth felt suddenly dry. This was the most unpredictable bunch of wild men north of the Fifty-third Parallel.

Sam Cocker—pioneer, orator, politician, ladies' man supreme, the first man to negotiate the then impassable trails from Ashcroft in southern British Columbia to Vanderhoof with a wagon.

Maynard Kerr—Vanderhoof's leading merchant, prospector, head of the Board of Trade, smooth as glass.

Pat Patterson—village blacksmith and Mayor, Irish iron man, keenest wit and deflator of egos and pomposity in the Pacific Northwest.

Skookum Davidson—legendary figure of northern British Columbia and the Yukon. Greatest packer of the day—a giant in strength with a voice that can be heard cannonading across a whole town, trained by yelling at pack trains and wild horses—a character who packs six-shooters, rounds up outlaws for the Northwest Mounted Police, and has busted up whole villages and frontier towns by himself.

"My God," I gasped at Bob Reid. "They didn't take me seriously did they?"

"Those boys are getting lined up this evening. What a time the gang of you are going to have down there in civilization. But your marriage—you might as well forget it."

Luckily for me one of my old friends, Ebert Lee, the son of a pioneer Vanderhoof family, who had founded and built up one of British Columbia's biggest truck and freight lines, Lee's Transport, arrived in town during the evening driving one of his giant new trailer trucks. I told Ebert the mess I had got myself into. We made plans, and long before daylight I jumped furtively into his truck and we roared towards Vancouver, leaving the best man and my ushers waiting happily for me in Pat Patterson's blacksmith shop.

Now my main objective, to marry Gloria, had been accomplished. We were back in Vanderhoof and I would have to face the group.

Our first caller was the fabulous Skookum Davidson. Now, instead of the booted and big-hatted giant with six-shooters hanging from his hip whom I had led Gloria to expect, the man who bowed graciously to her as he entered our hotel room was dressed in a dark pin-stripe suit, starched white shirt and quiet tie, and his ease of manner matched his immaculate garb.

Pat Patterson and Sam Cocker, Maynard Kerr and Bob Reid with their wives all arrived to pay their respects to my bride. Their manners were charming, their talk was interesting but not in the least disquieting.

"He has brought back a gracious and lovely bride," Bob Reid summed up, "and he did it without any help from us."

"But," said Gloria, "it will be a long time before I believe anything more that Rich tells me about the North Country and his Wild West friends."

Several days before we loaded up our food, horse feed and belongings on the sleigh and pack horses and headed for the mountains, the well-behaved Skook must have felt the pressure bearing down on his perfect behavior. He hired John Russ, one of the town's accordionists, to follow us about the village and into our quarters playing cowboy tunes. Skook even rented the thin-walled bedroom next to ours where he goaded the tired accordion player into playing from dark to dawn for two full nights.

The day we headed for Batnuni, Skook was also pushing off into the wilds in the direction of his horse ranch six hundred miles north of Vanderhoof to Lower Post on the Yukon boundary, and Gloria now had a chance to see the colorful horseman in the advertised regalia.

And then we were on our own with the dark snow-drifted forests closing in on the four-up and the pack horses.

Our small compact safari consisted first and foremost of the four-up. Mike and Bud, called the wheel team, were next to the sleigh box, and the leaders were Frankie and Toni. The wheelers or luggers are as a rule larger horses than the leaders who are picked more for agility and quickness on sharp turns. Mike and Bud were low, blocky animals, brown and gray, weighing around 1,700 pounds each. Frankie and Toni were a well-matched, leggy, quick-on-the-getaway team, weighing around 1,350 pounds apiece.

There were Stuyve and Nimpo, small half-Arab saddle horses, with quite a history in British Columbia; Skook, a long-faced, gentle running horse, a wedding present from Skook Davidson to Gloria and named after the donor; and there were my fast young trail bays, Rhino and Giant, 1,300 pounds, seventeen hands, long in the leg, short in the back, deep in the chest, fast walkers. Rhino was a good rope horse and almost unbeatable when it came to running wild range horses. Moonshine, Harold Dwinnell's Morgan-cross cow horse, rounded out the horses.

My trail companion, the Bear, a dark-colored, high-toned mongrel cow dog who never moved far from me, whether I was sleeping, eating, driving cattle or running horses, took up his usual scout position at the head of the cavalcade, his bushy tail used for balance carried high over his back, his ears flapping up and down. The sharp-nosed dog moved proudly but cautiously down the trail as if he were walking on eggshells, ignoring his girl friend, the Queen, a great affectionate cream and white Saint Bernard, who galloped happily back and forth, getting in everyone's way, scaring the horses and barking her enthusiasm now that the trip had started.

There had been speculation on Harold's and my part as to how the Bear would receive Gloria. If there was ever a jealous, one-man dog, he was it. So far he had merely eyed her curiously, then carried on with his own way of life, ignoring Gloria's existence entirely.

Harold's and Lucille's three children were with us. Charlie, a trim-built, freckle-faced, bright-eyed boy of eight who already could throw a wicked loop, rode Moonshine on this first day out of Vanderhoof. The two beautiful little blond, blue-eyed daughters, Colleen, six, and Darlene, three, rode up on top of the high sleigh with Gloria and their mother and their teamster father, while I rode Rhino.

It was now close to the first of February. Owing to deep snow and, later, mud, this seventy-five-mile sleigh road over the mountains would soon be impractical for hauling freight until well into May unless nature played a most unusual trick. It was absolutely essential to have all necessary food and equipment for four months loaded on this last sleigh trip of the season.

Such items as flour, sugar, beans, rice and macaroni,

salt, coffee and lard were essentials, but many other important items were on our lists. Some of the musts were harness leather, snaps, rings, latigo leather, soft ropes, hard-twist rope, glass panes, glass cutters, lamp gas, coal oil, sewing kit, smooth wire, horseshoes and nails, eight-to twelve-ounce canvas, ammunition, medical equipment, veterinary supplies and medicines, nuts and bolts of all sizes, burlap, raw wool to repair garments and make replacements, scrap iron of various sorts, sizes and shapes, necessary for repairs in a remote area where the horse and the vehicles he lugs and works are essential to operating a cow outfit, and of course there were always tools to be replaced and myriads of other articles that were constantly being used on the ranch and the range.

Harold had worked nearly two days on the inventory, figuring out just how much of this item and that would be used by each person on the ranch for at least 120 days, multiplied by the total of the population. Gloria was astounded at the careful preparation that went into the organization of our load.

She spoke to Harold as the sleigh slid along.

"Why, I always thought, read and saw in the movies that it was a simple matter for a cowboy to harness up his team and trot to town for a few supplies. Now it appears that foresight is a very important part of the ranch business."

"Git out of it, Toni," Harold called in a loud voice to the horse. "Step up there, you old knothead."

He crossed his empty right hand encased in teamster's gloves over to his left which held the four lines between thumb and next three fingers, all four lines dangling over his hand. Deftly he pulled one line slightly tighter and let two slip through his fingers for an inch or two.

"Toni," he barked.

The leggy gray broke forward to come even with Frankie and the lead stretchers tightened up again.

Harold was an expert four-up man, an art that takes a lot of driving practice, a lot of time to learn and no end of horse savvy. Now with the doubletrees and lead stretchers humming evenly in tension, Harold turned towards Gloria.

"The next time you drift over this trail, Gloria, you'll know a lot of the answers. There's a big difference in running a cow outfit which is cut off from the world for months at a time and the average outfit that's within reach of supplies.

"We're plenty far back in the toolies at Batnuni— seventy-five miles from a car road—but the Home Ranch, the main unit of the Frontier Company, where Panhandle Phillips is holed up for the winter feeding cows, is close to two hundred miles from town.

"Maybe you'll get up there next summer when we're moving cattle or horses between the units. If you do you'll see a real old-time cow outfit. The newspapers and magazines claim it's the most remote cattle ranch in North America, and I sure don't doubt that one bit."

"I'm not particularly anxious to go back any farther than the Batnuni," answered Gloria. "From what I hear of it, I'll be getting into an old-time cow outfit there too."

It was at this point that one of Gloria's cheeks turned from pink to paper white, and at the same time her left hand stopped hurting and went numb. Harold pulled the team to a stop and I rubbed the circulation back with my hands and a bit of snow. We made Gloria and Lucille and the children dance up and down and then walk behind the sleigh for a half mile to get blood stirring up.

Late on that frosty afternoon of Gloria's first day on the trail, our outfit broke suddenly out of the bushes on a long narrow clearing where several settlers had staked out land and were running a few beef cattle and milk cows, and raising excellent vegetable gardens. The Bear haughtily led the way towards an old weather-grayed log house, and a large log barn and corrals.

A collie dog ran towards our line-up yacking. The Queen stopped in her tracks waving her big bushy tail over her back as she said hello to the little collie who stopped his barking and smiled up at her. But the Bear paid not the slightest attention. He strutted on by the collie and the Queen and headed in the direction of the outbuildings. The Bear had been here many times before.

This was Elijah Hargreaves' homestead, at the edge of the mountain country where we often put up for the night, either coming or going between Batnuni and town. Lije was one of the earliest settlers in this part of the country and although he didn't run a stopping house, we were always welcome, and in return we bought potatoes, chickens and horse feed from him.

As Harold swung the team through the gate towards the barn a tall dark-skinned figure with thin black and gray side-whiskers and a long black goatee, stepped from the back porch and waved a walking stick in our direction. The man was wearing army pants with puttees. Heavy gray underwear and wide suspenders decorated his upper half. He paused there on the porch a moment, then ducked back into the house.

"Who is that?" exclaimed Gloria. "That man looks exactly like Haile Selassie."

"Charlie McHenry," I called to her as I jumped down from my horse. "There's a real character for you."

Harold brought the team to a stop and amidst the confusion of unloading freezables and taking care of the horses I tried briefly to describe Charlie.

Charlie was half Alabama Negro and half Oklahoma Cherokee Indian. He had pioneered in the country west of us and always claimed to be "the first white man in the Ootsa Lake Country."

His experiences were legendary. He was Elijah's permanent house guest and also tutor for Lije's small son, George. That's as far as I got in my description of McHenry.

Horses were tramping about blowing steam in the air. Kids and dogs were running here and there and Elijah arrived in our midst, a five-foot-tall, thoughtful, happy-go-lucky frontiersman.

Harold and I took care of the horses, then headed for the house. A pale pink and blue sky on the tree-lined eastern horizon told us we were in for a cold snap.

There was just enough room for the bunch of us to mill about Lije's iron heater in the small living room. We had no sooner settled ourselves when Charlie McHenry began to give Gloria and Lucille a blow-by-blow description of the ill-fated trip that he and Maynard Kerr and I had endured the year before, an unproductive seven-week foray with saddle and pack horses into the little-known Fawnie, Itcha and Nechako mountain ranges in search of strategic war minerals. It had been one of those expeditions when everything went wrong including our estimates of time and mileage and food requirements.

As we axed our way through a deadly, burned-over muskeggy country on the last two weeks of the journey we lived entirely on tobacco, coffee, three small suckers, several scrawny crows and two ground squirrels. Maynard wound up with a stomach ulcer, McHenry with a permanently crippled hip and myself with a loss of forty-five pounds and a phobia which haunts me to this day—a deadly fear that I will run out of food. As a result I have insisted on an overstocked stomach and pantry ever since.

CHAPTER II

A Strange New World

The night we spent with McHenry and Elijah and the following days on the bush trail to Batnuni were commonplace to me, but to Gloria, fresh from the city, every hour brought new and exciting experiences. So I'm turning this chapter over to my wife, whose recollections and impressions are aided by a diary she kept of her first days on the frontier.

THE WALLS IN MCHENRY'S and Elijah's living room had been covered with a flowered wallpaper that rippled in and out over the logs, and where the house had settled, the paper had ripped, exposing the logs and the insulation which consisted of old newspapers, egg cartons, wool underwear and worn-out socks tucked in between the cracks.

In the kitchen dark blue paper had been stretched over the logs, and it carried the grease stains and smoke smudges of many years. On the kitchen range sat an ancient coffeepot, a huge black kettle bubbling with some kind of chicken mash that gave off a sickish odor, and the remainder of the stove top was covered with eggshells and rust.

I began to worry about where we were all going to sleep, for a gray blanket hung over an opening in the living room disclosed that there was just one bedroom. But Rich solved that problem when he came in and announced happily that he had made up a bed for us in the hayloft in the barn.

During the day, while the sun was shining on the snow, it had seemed warm, but as soon as the sun dipped out of sight the cold frosty air closed in around us as we sorted out the freezables and moved them into the kitchen. A thermometer hung on the wall outside the kitchen door. It read ten below zero that night when Rich and I and the Queen and the Bear said good night and picked our way through some fallen-in corrals to the log barn which stood among a group of snow-covered spruce trees.

I started to giggle to myself. It was hard to believe that only a few days before I had worried about Rich having to share a bathroom with my brother in our house in Vancouver. Now, the nearest "bathroom" leaned lop-sidedly up against a chicken house, its door askew, and the moonlight shining in on the frost-covered mail-order catalog.

I have read a lot of lyrical descriptions of the joys of sleeping in a hayloft on the sweet-smelling hay. That night I decided that they were all written by people who had never had that experience. I was wearing an unbelievable amount of clothes, scratchy woolen underwear, wool slacks, a flannel shirt and Indian raw-wool sweater under my heavy canvas parka, and bulky Indian raw-wool socks in low-laced rubber boots with felt inner soles. That night I undressed to the extent of taking off the rubber boots and the parka, and some time during the night, as I tossed and struggled in the heavy sleeping bag, I seriously considered putting my parka on again, in the hope that the hood would prevent some of the hay and grain stalks and chaff from seeping down my neck.

Late the following morning I climbed wearily down the ladder on the outside of the barn to find that Rich and Harold had the sleigh loaded, the horses harnessed and saddled. Upon enquiring I was told my make-up kit was packed in the bottom of the sleigh. Lucille loaned me a lipstick and a comb, McHenry poured me a cup of coffee, I refused the pancakes which steamed in a large black frying pan next to the chicken mash, and almost before I had time to properly thank McHenry and Lije for their hospitality, Rich was hoisting me up onto Stuyve. The Dwinnell children climbed into the sleigh behind Lucille, Harold stood in the front of the sleigh, gathered up his four lines in his left hand, and shouted to his four big horses, and we were off for the Batnuni.

Directly in back of the house the trail climbed steeply up the face of a small mountain where seepage water had flowed out of the cut in the bank and formed an unmarked pale blue ice surface that tilted alarmingly towards the edge of the cliff. Rich rode his big bay Rhino and led Skook ahead of me.

He yelled at me—"Kick your feet out of the stirrups coming across here, and if Stuyve slips, roll off on the upside of him."

I let the little bay pick his way carefully across the icy face, keeping my head averted so that I couldn't see the sheer drop to the tiny creek at the bottom of the hill.

When we were safely at the top we turned and watched the four horses pulling the sleigh up. The lead horses seemed to step easily across the ice, but the wheelers, Mike and Bud, dug in and pulled with their bellies almost touching the ground. We waved to Lije and McHenry who stood like toy figures beside the creek, then swung around the hill.

Ahead of us a cone-shaped, treeless, snow-smothered mountain called Sinkut rose up. As the trail leveled off and swung towards its lower slopes, the snow deepened. Slowly, so slowly, we plodded along the trail which wound gradually around the mountain. Off to the south an unbroken endless panorama of green jackpines stretched away to a cloudless cold horizon.

Charlie Dwinnell waved to me and then to the south— "The Batnuni is over there, Gloria. We'll be there in four or five days."

It must have been about one o'clock in the afternoon when Rich reined Rhinoceros in under a giant spruce tree. I dismounted stiffly, the cords in the back of my legs felt as if they were on fire, but as I floundered about in the snow gathering up twigs and sticks for our noon campfire, my legs gradually loosened up again.

Harold unhitched his four-up, took the bits out of their mouths and poured little piles of oats for each of them on sacks placed on the snow. Rich did the same for the saddle horses. Lucille dug a large tin with a wire handle out of the kitchen box, filled it with snow and set it over the fire. Our sandwiches were frozen but we ate ravenously, drank many steaming mugs of coffee, and within an hour were on our way again.

We were to travel about twenty miles this day to the Halfway Cabin. As the sun disappeared and my legs stiffened up again and the cold air crept insidiously inside my parka, I kept my mind fastened optimistically on the thought of the cabin. Visions of a great open fire, hot food and soft beds swam in my mind. I could hardly believe it when we turned a bend in the trail and faced a ramshackle log building which couldn't have stood over six feet in height, and measured about eight by eight feet in size.

Inside it a crude pole bunk was built into one corner, but in place of a mattress, great piles of twigs and pine cones and shredded bits of cardboard lay piled on it. Another heap of rubbish sat on the top of a tiny tin stove.

"Oh, darn it," said Lucille. "Those pack rats have moved in again."

She grabbed up the remains of a broom which leaned against the windowless log wall and began to sweep the refuse out the plank door into the snow. For the first time, I smelled the unforgettable unpleasant odor of pack rats, the greatest nuisance in the North Country.

Rich carried our kitchen box into the tiny cabin and Lucille set to work to cook up a dinner for the group of us. She worked quickly and efficiently. Before very long, soup from a series of packages bubbled on the camp stove, and a great frying pan held a luscious golden-brown bannock, a giant sort of fluffy biscuit.

Fortunately Rich seemed to dislike the pack-rat odor as much as I did, and immediately after supper, while we waited for the snow water to melt to wash out tin plates and mugs, he lugged our sleeping bags and several canvases out in the snow, and made up our beds under the wide branches of a spruce.

I was watching him make up the beds when I heard the distant tinkle of sleigh bells. I listened for a long time before I said anything, for I had been told that the only people in the country other than ourselves were the Goodlands, a Scotch-English family who had home-steaded some thirty miles beyond the Halfway Cabin.

The stars were flashing through the tall tops of the spruce trees which seemed to be bending under the weight of the snow on their branches, whitish smoke curled up from the stovepipe which shoved crookedly through the roof of the little cabin, when a sleigh drawn by four frost-covered horses, whose breath showed white and steamy in the cold air, drew up in front of the cabin.

A man and woman sat in the front of the sleigh. The man wore a high fur hat like a Russian Cossack's, and a heavy moosehide jacket with long fringes. The girl's pretty face peeped out of a fur-lined parka, her dark eyes sparkling.

They sat for a minute without speaking and the scene was exactly like a Currier and Ives print. It was almost too good to be true.

It was, indeed, the Goodlands, the younger couple, on their way to town for supplies.

Lucille and the children tumbled out of the low door of the cabin, and suddenly everybody was talking at once. I was introduced to Sam Goodland, a tall, quiet, serious-faced man in his thirties, and his vivacious tiny wife, Jean, who was obviously still in her teens.

The Goodlands moved their bedrolls into the cabin with the Dwinnells. I worried a little about where they were all going to sleep before I fell asleep myself with the Queen snuggled up against me. The Bear was on the far side of the bed next to Rich. He was still very aloof. Sometimes I would catch him looking at me speculatively, but whenever he noticed me looking his way he would turn his head and walk self-consciously off.

The barking of the dogs woke me. The Queen was standing with her hind feet on my stomach, her 130 pounds shifting back and forth across my body as she excitedly tried to climb the spruce we were sleeping under. High in the branches a tiny chipmunk chattered saucily. The sun on my face was hot, and the reflection of it on the snow sparkled like millions of diamonds. It was a beautiful morning.

I crawled out of my sleeping bag expecting to be stiff and sore, but I only felt a tremendous feeling of well-being. The nights in the open air, the exercise and the excitement of the unexpected were doing their work. In the city I led an average life, and was used to arising in the morning with the city feeling—tired, not too excited about what was ahead of me, and feeling the effects of too-late nights, too many cigarettes and a life spent largely within walls.

That morning, I received an inkling of what it was like to live in the open. I still am amazed, on bush trips to wake up with that completely rested, revitalized feeling, even though the night before when I crawled into bed I was so physically tired I thought I would never be able to get up again.

That day we traveled ten miles to the 44 Camp, where a tiny frozen stream meandered along beside a high log fence which enclosed about ten acres of willow bottom and open wild meadow. This was one of the Frontier Cattle Company holding pens, and was used as a night holding pasture on the beef drives from the Frontier ranches to Vanderhoof and the railroad.

We had had slow going that day. We had reached the height of land, 4,100 feet, and the snow lay nearly three feet deep in the bush. The unevenly broken trail was rough, and the four-up had to rest many times during the day. Only once had we seen an opening, and that was a great muskeg with tiny stunted Christmas trees sprouting here and there across its broad expanse, only the very tops of their branches showing above the white blanket.

We made a comfortable camp. Near the stream several big jackpine trees had been ringed and the bark peeled off them with an axe by Rich. They were now dry, and yellow with pitch, and our campfire blazed and sputtered cheerfully in front of the little pup tent where the children slept. Lucille and Harold, like Rich and me, had simply stretched their bedrolls out on top of canvases under spruce trees. The horses were turned loose in the log enclosure and they pawed away at the deep snow, nibbling at the high, coarse edged wild slough grass which they uncovered.

Lucille fried bacon and hotcakes over the campfire. The Queen sat next to me and begged incessantly throughout the meal, but the Bear lay a short distance from our camp with his back turned to us. He had followed Rich for many years along the trails; sometimes they had been short of food, and the Bear had devised his own trail etiquette. He never begged on the trail. In a house it was different. He knew that there was usually a good supply of food in a house, and he was not embarrassing anyone by asking for it.

The next night, long after dark, we twisted and turned down a long hill to a neat little valley where the Goodlands had their homestead. Beautifully constructed log buildings were dotted about in the tall trees bordering the river which wound through their meadow.

Sam's father, Harry, a slim, aristocratic-looking Englishman, came out to meet us, swinging a coal-oil lantern. He led the horses to the barn while Lucille and the children and I walked to the house, a new log structure some thirty feet by twenty feet. The door was open and the heavenly smell of new-baked bread streamed out. Inside, Mrs. Goodland, a gray-haired, jolly Scotswoman with a hearty laugh and a witty tongue, was setting the table in a big cozy kitchen. The dim coal-oil light threw shadows across the huge iron cookstove, the blue-willow-pattern china and the homemade patchwork quilts which covered the cots in the roomy, square living room. The house was warm and cheerful and, once inside, it was hard to believe that it was sitting all by itself in an immensity of forests where the only neighbors were the squirrels, the mink and fisher and otter that traversed the little wilderness creeks, and the moose and coyotes and wolves and grizzly bears that inhabited the wild meadows and heavy bush.

That night we slept on feather mattresses and woke to the cheery sounds of a fire crackling in the big oil-drum heater in the living room. Before many minutes had passed, Harry knocked on the partition that divided our bedroom from the living room and then entered carrying a cup of tea for me. A breakfast of feathery Scotch scones, wild blueberry jam and tea, and we waved good-bye to the old couple who stood together under the trees in front of the house.

The Goodlands had moved to their wild meadow several years before, and while Sam and Jean made the occasional sleigh and pack-horse trip out to town for supplies and mail, the older couple had only been out to civilization once in two years. But they showed no signs of the isolated life they led. Their battery radio supplied them with all the news of the world and what was going on in it, they were keen and interested in all the up-to-the-minute happenings, well read and, above all, relaxed and contented in the little empire of their own building. In the old country Harry had been trained as a carpenter, and his early training was evident in many things; the hand-wrought iron door latches, the neat dovetail corners of the log buildings, and the free-swinging, handsome log gates set in the numerous worm fences and corrals around their place.

All that day we traveled through heavy spruce trees on a trail so narrow that the sun was obscured by their tall tops. Filmy clouds of north-slope gray moss hung from the trees giving the whole landscape a ghostly appearance. We were still traveling when the moon came up, throwing weird shadows across the trail. Rich and I rode on ahead of the sleigh to Marvin Lake which was to be our night camp. As we trotted through an area which had been burned over, and where snow-covered stumps and half-burned logs leaned grotesquely in every direction, Rich casually remarked,

"This is great wolf country."

My hair practically stood on end. At that time I didn't
know enough about the ferocious northern wolf to
realize that he was a wary creature, suspicious of man-
smell and man-made things, and that the chances of
seeing one of them, or a pack, was very unlikely. I didn't
mention my fears to Rich, but in my imagination each
strange-shaped log took on the appearance of a wolf. I
was greatly relieved when Rich reined up beside a log
corral, and announced that we would make camp. It
wasn't till a great windfall fire threw its sparks high into
the air, that I was able to relax, and even then I fancied
that I saw dark shapes hovering about just outside of the
rim of firelight waiting to pounce on me.

It was while we were making breakfast the next
morning that Harold called me over to look at some marks
on a spruce tree. They were about fourteen feet off the
ground, great gashes in the bark. These were grizzly-bear
teeth marks made while the monstrous bear had stood on
his hind feet. The area around Marvin Lake, a muddy
pothole with lily pads growing almost solidly over its dull
surface in the summer, was the headquarters of a breed of
gigantic grizzly bears. They roamed the gloomy country
extending back to the Tatuk Mountains which we could
barely make out to the west of us.

The more I hear about grizzlies, the more respect I
have for them. They are the kings of the woods. They
are so used to having their own way, all other animals
giving them a wide berth, that they have no fear of man,
and should a person surprise one of these mountainous
proud animals, they want to realize that a grizzly con-
siders the trail is his. He is not afraid of anything.

As Harold related some of the stories about the Tatuk Mountain grizzlies that morning, I was glad that I hadn't heard about them the night before, and had only the relatively harmless-to-humans wolves to think and worry about.

We broke camp, and once again rode down the dark narrow trail. It was about noon when we climbed a little hill and then, suddenly, we were on the top of it, looking out at a wide-open prairie where only a few gigantic poplar trees, their bark pale and colorless, stretched up out of the snow into a warm blue sky. It was as if we had come out of a dark room into the sunlight.

We reined in our horses and sat for a few minutes looking silently out at the valley which lay before us. Wide, with gently rolling hills sloping down to a great lake with poplar and pine-covered islands.

"Batnuni Valley," said Rich.

"It's beautiful," I said.

Rich looked pleased. "Just the beginning of it. These open hills go on for miles in each direction. We're just ten miles from the ranchhouse now."

We rode along the edge of the lake for several miles, and at the end of it came to a tiny log cabin with blue smoke curling lazily out from the crooked stovepipe.

"Old Bill Comstock lives here," explained Rich as we rode up to the cabin door. "He built this cabin after he sold us the Batnuni Ranch. He does a little trapping in the winter. You'll get a kick out of Uncle Bill. He's quite a character. Looks as if he's home today."

Before Rich had finished speaking the cabin door opened. A man who stood at least six feet four inches in his bedroom slippers, and must have weighed at least 250 pounds shouted hello at Rich, and then raised one white eyebrow and looked at me quizzically.

"I'll be damned," he drawled, in a flat, American, Rocky Mountain accent, after Rich explained who I was.

"Well come in, come in," he said, "I can only offer you a drink of home brew, but this batch is pretty good."

We slid down off our horses and stepped into the cabin. It was small, with three tiny windows, but was immaculate.

Behind a built-in bunk stretched three six-foot-long bookshelves, neatly piled with interesting-looking, well-worn books. A new combination heater–cookstove stood against one wall, the pots and pans hanging behind it were shining and spotless. On the other side of the cabin was a built-in table, and in the corner a wash stand.

It was a good batch of beer, almost as good as the homemade taffy Uncle Bill handed me.

I had one uncomfortable moment when Comstock suddenly snapped at Rich in an irritable voice that he, Rich, had hung the dipper up on the wrong nail.

Rich hurriedly changed the tin dipper over into its correct position.

Later, as we rode toward the Batnuni ranchhouse I asked Rich about the incident. He explained to me that Uncle Bill had an advanced case of cabin fever. Witty and agreeable as he was out of his cabin, once in it, he became as fussy as the proverbial old maid. Everything had to be just so. However, this form of housekeeping cabin fever I later decided was preferable to the other extreme a lot of people living alone in the bush went to—that was just letting things go. Living alone, and having no chance to make comparisons, can result in a sloppiness that is almost unbelievable to an outsider.

It was growing dark when we rode through a gate in a high log fence and saw ahead of us scattered buildings, corrals and the happy glow of a light in a new, two-story, gabled house which sat on a hill surrounded by poplar and spruce trees.

Through another gate, and off to the side, sat a long low log cabin with windows all around it.

"We'll go to the ranchhouse first and you can warm up while I get the fire going in our cabin," said Rich.

We rode up to the new house. A tall well-built man in his late twenties limped out to greet us, his face was split by a grin that stretched from ear to ear. Quiet, good-humored Jack Lee had been alone at the Batnuni for the past month, but when I stepped into the ranchhouse I noticed that it was as neat as if a woman had been cleaning it regularly. A big oil-drum heater roared in the living room. At one end of the bright, many-windowed room stood a long table covered with yellow oilcloth. There was little furniture in the room. Just two obviously homemade settees, and three old-fashioned rocking chairs around the heater.

In the kitchen stood an old-fashioned wood stove, and on its top bubbled a pot of potatoes and a saucepanful of applesauce, and sitting on a side table was a batch of newly baked baking-powder biscuits.

"Sure glad you're back." Jack grinned. "Was gettin' kind of tired of eating my own grub."

After sampling some of Jack's good strong coffee, and complimenting him on his biscuits, I hurried over to the cabin where I would be living for the next year.

Rich had a fire going in the heater in the big square living room, and two coal-oil lights threw wavering reflections on the many windows, the high-beamed pole ceiling, and the bear and cougar skin rugs on the floor. Off the living room were two bedrooms, small, with just room enough for their double log beds, a cupboard and some rough shelves for clothes.

The Queen and the Bear were already stretched out on their separate bear rugs, occasionally groaning contentedly, and two runted pearl-gray kittens purred and rubbed themselves against Rich's legs. Rich introduced them to me as PeeWee and Grandma.

We cooked ourselves up another cup of coffee on the heater, I mentally hung curtains at the windows and, finally, stretching tired muscles and luxuriating in the thought that I could sleep in the next morning, I fell asleep. We were home.

Every day at the Batnuni was exciting to me. There were none of the grueling, day-by-day boring chores that I always associated with farming.

Each day began when I heard Rich roll out of bed and start the fire in the heater. Sometimes when I poked my nose out of the covers I would see that the windows were covered with frost, and when I breathed into the bedroom my breath formed a blue haze. But the smell of coffee would bring me up and out of bed in a rush.

Breakfast over at the ranchhouse—great stacks of hotcakes and butter and syrup, and more coffee along with the discussion of what the men would do that day. Jack and Harold would already have fed and harnessed the work teams and saddled up horses for the day's work.

The ranch was enormous. It seemed to ramble all over the country. It took me a while to adjust to the size of it. One morning I took a ride on the hay sleigh out to the calf pen, which was nearly a mile from the ranch buildings. Hundreds of blocky, whitefaced Hereford calves played and ate inside a huge log enclosure. They drank out of holes that the men opened in the ice of a little creek that flowed through the corral, and slept under the boughs of a great stand of spruce trees. Even on a bitterly cold day, when the wind on the open meadow would cut through the warmest clothes, it was quiet and warm and protected under the spruce. Rich explained that he preferred to have the strong beef animals sheltered by the spruce instead of in sheds, as the animals would bunch up in a shed, and sudden changes of temperature were harder on them than keeping an even temperature out in the trees.

So many people just can't believe that cattle can winter out in the open at temperatures of fifty and sixty below zero. As the temperature goes down it is necessary to feed the cattle more hay, and when the coldest weather hits, the animals have feed in front of them all the time. They keep walking, and eating. The principle is the same as stoking a furnace.

The big mother herd of cows was fed off in another meadow, and also sheltered under spruce. The most pampered animals on the ranch were the bulls, great, blocky, gentle whitefaces, who lounged around in a sheltered feedyard, received the best of the hay, would stand for hours scratching themselves on an uneven rail in the fence, or lie chewing their cud in the sun.

The Hereford bull, unlike most bulls of other breeds, is a gentle animal. On a well-run ranch they are the most important animals on the place, always registered, and usually bought in a show ring. On the other hand, the Hereford cows who run on the range are apt to be wild. They take very seriously their job of protecting their calves from coyotes, bears, wolves or strange people. All the cow work at Batnuni was done by men on saddle horses, and the sight of a person on foot would send the cow herd running in every direction.

One day Rich asked me to go along with him to a wild meadow called the Pennoyer Meadow, where several stacks of bluejoint hay were to be fed out to the cows. He wanted to go up himself and open the water holes for the first time.

The several hundred cows were eating contentedly at scattered piles of sweet-smelling hay when we tied our saddle horses to two jackpine trees and walked across an open meadow to the frozen creek. Rich started to chop out holes which resembled long bathtubs in the ice. They can't be so wide that animals will fall into them, but of necessity have to be long and narrow. If the water level is low in the creek, steps in the ice are cut so that the animals can walk easily down and reach the water. Rich explained that if an animal is to come through the winter in good thrifty shape it must have lots of water along with its dry hay.

Rich was chopping away industriously, and I was trying to roll a cigarette, something I found I had to learn on a cattle ranch, not only for economic and social reasons, but because the practice of smoking tailormades (which retained their hot ash longer) was frowned on around haystacks, straw-filled barns and tinder-dry hayfields.

I suddenly looked up and found myself staring into a ring of curious faces. Some two hundred head of cows had left their hay and had silently and cautiously crept up to us. They were standing three and four deep around us, all their heads turned in, their long narrow-pointed horns contrasting in a sinister way with their innocent white faces and brownish-red necks.

I called to Rich who straightened up and said in a low voice, "Should have noticed them—they are just thirsty—but don't make any fast movement."

Rich started to whistle and talk to the cows. Then he turned to me and said,

"Walk right behind me—they're really all right but sometimes one damn fool will make a quick move and all the rest will follow."

We walked slowly towards one group of cows who reluctantly backed away a few steps, pushing against the cows behind them. Rich waved his axe and the bunch threw up their heads and backed away again. Then they stood perfectly still and watched us walk slowly across the wide meadow to where our horses were tied.

"Range cows are usually pretty quiet around the feedyard in the winter," explained Rich, as I hurriedly mounted my saddle horse. "They will leave a person afoot alone when they haven't got their calf to worry about, but sometimes when they ring you that way, a wild one will make a bad move. But you can usually tell by the look in their eye."

As hard as I have tried since, I never seem to be able to distinguish between a range cow with a good look in her eye or a bad one. I just assume they're all wild and act accordingly.

A few days after my encounter with the wild cows Rich asked me to ride with him the sixteen miles to the McNutt place (a deserted homestead) to check on the "wild band." The wild band was the horse herd which was turned loose and ran at large over the country, rustling out for their winter feed on the numerous pothole slough-grass meadows that dotted the range country. The mares and their colts, the as-yet-unbroken yearlings, two- and three-year-old horses, and any of the work or saddle stock which were not needed at the ranch, made up the wild band.

We rode down past the frozen Batnuni and Comstock lakes, our breath and that of the horses wisping out as blue smoke in the frosty air.

At the turnoff to Vanderhoof, we struck east along the frozen Batnuni River which alternately dipped through canyons and meandered along through poplar parks. Rich described the wonderful rainbow trout fishing to be found in this little river in the summertime, but with the temperature hovering at about ten below, it was a little difficult for me to visualize the wild flowers, the deep pools that formed along the river, and the excitement of hooking into a big one.

It was early afternoon when we rode out onto the McNutt flat, a swampy meadow where three-foot-high green slough grass pushed through the snow. A herd of some sixty horses were pawing at the grass. When they saw us, they stopped as if they were one animal and threw their heads in the air to watch us. As we slowly rode up they swung in a large circle and galloped away into the windfall that bordered the opening. Rich yelled at me—"Stay right here—" before he swung Rhino in behind them. And then he too disappeared.

I was riding Stuyve. The little half-Arabian was a sociable animal who hated to be left alone, and as soon as he realized he had been deserted by the other horses he started to dance and prance across the meadow. Occasionally he would lower his head suggestively, and I would hurriedly rein him around in a circle and throw him off balance so that he couldn't start to buck. I had heard enough early-morning breakfast conversations around the table at Batnuni to realize that when a horse downed his head he was preparing to "unload his rider."

I untied the cords of the hood of my heavy parka and pushed it back, hoping I would be able to hear horse bells. But even they had vanished, so I knew that Rich and the wild band were already a good distance away from the little meadow where Stuyve and I waited anxiously. A fine snow whistled around us as we waited. It seemed to emphasize the awesome loneliness of the country. East of us, about twenty-five miles away, was one family, the Hills, who ranched on the Nazko trail. The Goodlands were some thirty-five miles north of us, and sixteen miles away, the Batnuni, with its comforting heaters and cozy cabins, was the only pinpoint of habitation in the great empty area that stretched from

McNutt's nearly two hundred miles west to the Pacific Coast.

It must have been an hour before I heard the sound of sticks and windfalls cracking, as Rich rode up.

"I had a look at them," he said. "They're all in good shape except a couple of black mares that have ticks. Harold and I will come down in a couple of days and cut them out and bring them in to the ranch. We'll have to put some coal oil on them to get rid of those ticks."

The early northern night dropped down on us long before we reached Batnuni, and for the next few days I was quite content to stay close to the ranchhouse.

Lucille volunteered to teach me how to make bread. This was a major operation. The only yeast which would keep through the long months and the fluctuating temperatures was the little hard cakes of Royal yeast. Breadmaking took two days. The first day the yeast was set to soak with some sugar and warm water, and when it began to bubble it was mixed with more warm water, shortening and enough flour to make a soft sponge. This mixture was kept overnight close to the heater—but not too close, for if the sponge became overheated it would collapse. By the same token, if it cooled off too much it was useless. The next morning one kneaded flour and salt into the sponge, set it in a warm place to rise, pounded it down, and generally by late afternoon the dough would be ready to make into buns and loaves.

Several times I watched Lucille produce delicious loaves and buns, and then one fatal day she told me that this time I was on my own. I started the yeast, wrapped it up carefully in my parka before I went to bed, and the following day hovered over the dough, peeking, poking and praying. Late in the afternoon I drew the great golden crusty loaves out of the oven and set them to cool. I was so excited by my success I grabbed one loaf and ran the half mile to the corrals where the men were working. As I puffed up to the fence, exclaiming and pointing to my work of art, Harold straightened up from his work of tying up a hind foot on a mare and said, "You gave me a bit of a scare, Gloria—I thought with all the excitement that you had produced a baby!"

But that night at dinner, the quiet, uncommunicative Jack Lee made up for it when he took a large slice of my bread, munched on it thoughtfully, and then pronounced it—"Good punk!"

So much for the woman stuff. Now to explain this layout in which Gloria found herself.

CHAPTER III

Bush Trip

THE ORIGINAL PLAN of the Frontier Cattle Company called for nine operating units strung for 130 miles from one meadow to another, all connected by wagon and sleigh roads, which we built ourselves. Each unit was shaped up to winter two hundred to four hundred head of grown stock. The number of cattle to be fed was determined by the amount of winter feed available on the different units. It took from one to two tons of hay to carry a cow through the winter.

In the spring and early summer most of the hay-meadow winter units would be closed up and cattle moved to either the Batnuni beef range or the breeding range in the Itcha Mountains, behind the Home Ranch.

The nine units were all much the same, with the exception of Panhandle Phillips' main headquarters at the Home Ranch and mine at the Batnuni. Pan was my original partner in this whole enterprise. At each of the other units we built a single-room log cabin, equipped with stove, heater and beds to accommodate three men, a ten-horse barn, a small food cache on stilts, a screened meat house and a privy. Each had a corral system with shute and squeeze, and a log horse-pasture which adjoined corrals and in most instances enclosed from four to eight acres of good grass. Roads were slashed into the units which included Tommy Meadow, Alexi Meadow, Purple Mountain Camp, Rich Meadow, Irene Rich Lake, Pan Meadow, the Mc-Nutt place, Upper Pan Meadow and Pennoyer Meadow.

It was a very workable and practical system of connecting ranches, capable of running 3,000 head of cattle, but when World War II broke out, ranch hands became unobtainable, and capital to develop the Company was cut off. Pan and I as managers of our respective units were left with heavy bank loans.

It was a sad deal. With reduced crews, instead of being able to stock our newly built units to capacity, we were forced to cut into our foundation herd of 1,200 head of well-bred cows and their calves which had been trailed in with considerable trouble, trail them back out to market and sell at a loss to pay off loans.

Consequently when Gloria arrived at Batnuni only the Home Ranch and the Batnuni and their closest hay meadows were in operation. All the other units were closed down.

It was nearly the end of February when I decided that I would hitch up Mike and Bud, and with Jack Lee as helper, break trail to the Pan Meadow some fifty-five miles away to pick up various tools, mowing machines, rakes, etc., which could be put to use at Batnuni the following summer.

Gloria wanted to see the Pan Meadow and all the wild country that sprawled out between it and Batnuni. The weather was bright and clear and not too cold, so Jack Lee and I decided to take her along.

Had we known what lay ahead of us along the snow-bound trail to Pan Meadow, Gloria would never have been allowed to go. On this trip into the back reaches of the Blackwater, she was to have her first contact with the bleak cold tragedy that so often strikes without warning on the remote edges of a frontier.

We built a long narrow hayrack on the sleigh bunks for the horse feed and equipment. Harold helped us load up the camp outfit, grub, hay and a sack of grain, and with the Bear following in our sleigh tracks, Gloria sitting happily and expectantly on the high mound of hay, Mike and Bud plunged into their traces and the sleigh skidded and whined out of the Batnuni Ranch.

The lakes were frozen hard. There were not many air holes to spot and glide around. I turned the lines over to Jack and we took to the lake. Mike and Bud, both sharp shod and raring to go, tried to break into a run, but Jack held them back to a fast walk. Big horses, those weighing over 1,600 pounds, should never trot or run with their load. Loping or running is for lighter faster teams, not for the big heavy luggers we kept for freighting at Batnuni.

Seven miles down the lakes we pulled up in front of Uncle Bill Comstock's cabin. Bill walked out onto the ice to greet us.

"Waal," he said, putting his mischievous grin to work. "The little lady here is going to need some kind of intelligent conversation on this trip. I guess I better come along."

Bill asked Gloria what kind of books she liked. A few minutes later he walked out of his cabin with an armful of books, his bedroll and an assortment of homemade pickles and other delicacies that Mrs. Comstock was famous for.

Mrs. Comstock lived in the town of Quesnel, 130 miles to the east of us.

Just before dark Jack drew the team up in front of one of the Company unit cabins, the McNutt place. Uncle Bill and Gloria went into the one-room log cabin to start the fire, and Jack and I took care of the team and packed up a couple of buckets of water from the creek.

I wasn't particularly surprised to find two Indian families occupying the cabin. George Alec, Zalowie George and their Indian wives often used the little cabin when tending their trap lines. These neat, good-mannered young Indians were great friends of mine, and through the preceding years had been on any number of good and bad trails with me. I had always been welcome in their homes at Trout Lake and Pelican Lake.

We greeted each other with handshakes, back poundings and shouts. I was delighted to introduce them to Gloria. But I noticed that they completely ignored Comstock. Uncle Bill didn't get along too well with these Indians, the reason being that they owned adjoining traplines. The resulting mix-ups had done little to help friendships through the years.

The one-room cabin was not quite spacious enough to accommodate seven adults, but at least it was not overly crowded by furniture. There was an old upside-down barrel heater whose top kept falling down into the fire, a four-by-four axe-hewn table and various orange crates holding tin dishes and pans and cracked mugs. Chairs consisted of hand-sawed log butts.

Gloria and the Indian women collaborated on the meal. Zalowie and Alec furnished freshly caught rainbow trout whose hard firm meat was dark red and fat. The Frontier Company threw in rice and spuds and Comstock brought out a large jar of mustard-and-vinegar pickles.

After a happy dinner the men retired to the den, in this case the horse barn, where we watered the horses and stacked up their separate piles of hay.

Gloria had been trying all evening to figure out how she was going to undress and slip into our sleeping bag over in one corner of the room in front of Jack Lee, the white-bearded Comstock and the assorted Indians who were now all comfortably ensconced in the cabin. The whole situation must have seemed ludicrous to her, but Uncle Bill solved her problem. He gallantly offered Gloria his services, which consisted of holding up a blanket as a curtain for her while she crawled into her pajamas and the bedroll.

Mike and Bud lugged the sleigh to Dry Lake the next day where we made a comfortable little camp on a pine-clad knoll overlooking a slough-grass meadow where the horses could paw through the snow for green grass to add to their daily rations of hay and grain.

The weather stayed its sunny best and Gloria picked up a nice fresh suntan on her face and arms as she stretched out on top of the load reading Jane Austen for the tenth time.

The following day Comstock remarked on the weather as he ran his hands along his back and various other previously injured parts of his anatomy.

"It's clamping down on us," he drawled. "I feel it in my bones. By tomorrow morning we'll be heading into a blizzard."

"That's right," agreed Jack Lee. "My bad leg is sure acting up."

Jack had been kicked down and tromped by a bronc years before, leaving him with many broken bones and one short leg.

Gloria shook her head as she picked out another of Comstock's books to read during the day that lay before us.

"I just can't imagine really bad weather striking us now. Everything is so warm and nice, the sky is blue and the sun is shining. I've always heard that here in the interior you have lots of warning before storms settle down."

"Let's get going," I barked. "Sundogs today—look up there. Ring around an upside-down moon last night, a damn wet-looking moon, and the moon is due to change today or tomorrow."

"Look at the Bear rolling around in the snow, and the horses playing," said Jack.

"There's a storm acoming and a real bad one at that," whined Comstock.

The trail swung almost due west from Dry Lake on the Titetown Lake crossing. It was an old Indian and fur trader's trail that, according to legend, followed Alexander Mackenzie's first crossing by land to the Pacific Ocean at Bella Coola in 1793. One fork of the trail swung southeast at right angles towards the Nazko Indian village some thirty miles away and the town of Quesnel about ninety miles distant.

As Jack Lee put the team westward into the parklike slopes of the Poplar Mountains, a snow-covered dreamlike land of tremendous poplar trees, I could see that only one team and sleigh had broken the trail before the last big snow some two weeks before. I knew who it was. Mrs. Hill and her daughter Gertie had gone into their hay camp to feed a small bunch of cattle.

Mrs. Hill was the great-granddaughter of a pioneer Mexican named Garcia. Nearly a hundred years before Garcia had arrived in the canyon town of Ashcroft with one of the first mule teams to reach lower British Columbia. Mrs. Hill was black-haired, black-eyed, dark-skinned, plumpish, yet well set together. She loved company and entertaining.

Gertie could do as much work as the average man. She resembled her happy-faced mother in appearance, had sparkling white teeth and black eyes that danced with health and good spirits.

Each winter the Hill women left old white-bearded Mr. Hill on their homestead near the Trout Lake Indian village and came up to this mountain meadow in the Poplar Mountains to feed their sixty or seventy head of cattle.

At dark we left the main trail and drove out onto the narrow little Hill meadow that cut through a stand of heavy spruce. In the distance the tiny dirt-roofed cabin and barn stood forlorn and ramshackle against the white forests surrounding them. The crudely made barn was too low-roofed to lead any of the company horses into, but was just right for the Hills' little ponies.

Uncle Bill and Gloria walked to the cabin where Gertie welcomed them. Jack Lee and I led the team into a rambling stackyard. A small snow-covered haystack graced its center. We unharnessed the team, let them roll, then tied them to the fence and forked out their evening's hay.

When Jack and I bent through the flimsy little door into the ten-by-twelve-foot cabin, we found Mrs. Hill lying on one of the cabin bunks.

"I think Mother worked too hard pitching hay out of an iced stack to the cattle the other day," Gertie said. "She's had a pain in her chest and she has trouble breathing."

"I'll be all right," Mrs. Hill said. "The only trouble is, we haven't been able to get out to the Indian store in Nazko to get any supplies for over three weeks. But Gertie shot a moose down the meadow and we've still got a hundred of flour."

I followed Gloria's startled glance to the far side of the room. Two obviously axe-butchered hindquarters of a moose hung from the pole ceiling at the foot of the bunk. Blood dripped on part of the bed. A cat was licking up the little hummocks of dried blood that hadn't run through the wide cracks in the floor. Another cat was curled up asleep in the opened top of the sack of flour. His freshly flour-powdered side whiskers and face gave him the look of a little old man.

Gertie and Gloria kept up a steady stream of conversation. They were pals right away. Uncle Bill filled in the gaps with remarks and wisecracks. Jack Lee sat on the floor by the old rusty cookstove staring, first at Gertie, and then at the dripping moose quarters and happy cats.

Gertie made a sudden very fast move. She jumped across Comstock's outstretched legs and grabbed up a long butcher knife from a rickety pole table. Jack cringed back against the wall.

She laughed. "I plumb forgot that you people must be hungry."

She slammed a large tin frying pan half filled with moose grease to the center of the stove. A few drops of the warm grease spattered onto Jack Lee's hat which luckily for him he hadn't removed from his head.

Gertie straddled Comstock's feet and started slashing away at a quarter of moose. A small chunk of blood and fat fell on Comstock's mop of white hair and trickled down on his beard.

"Ouch," he said. "Covering me with raw meat. I want to eat the steaks, not take a bath in 'em."

Gertie slashed off several more steaks, stepped on Comstock's foot and dripped more blood over the old man's hair and mackinaw coat. She yelled at him—

"Serves you right, you lazy old fool, sitting there with your big fat carcass in everybody's way."

Gertie bounded to the stove with the steaks and Jack rolled quickly out of the way.

"Steaks for all," Gertie yelled. And into the pan they splashed with a loud squishing swooshy noise.

"None for me," Gloria said. "Nothing at all for me. I'm not hungry."

Gloria's face was a kind of pale green and she looked as if she wanted to be sick. I wondered what was the matter with her. The only thing that bothered me about the present setup was the smell of rendered and several times re-cooked moose grease—a ghastly odor. But I took my steak up and ate it outside the cabin where I studied the sky which was now overcast and the general feel of the weather that was closing in on us.

Very fine, almost indiscernible flakes of snow touched me on the cheek. A faint wind, bone-chilling but wet by the feel of it, gently rustled the tall pines around the cabin. Cattle had assembled around the little stackyard and the air was filled with their anguished bawls. I knew they weren't getting enough hay but I also knew that the obstinate Gertie was taking the chance that she could pull the herd through on what little hay they had in the stack.

Gertie and Gloria slept together on one bunk. Mrs. Hill slept in the other, and Comstock and I rolled some blankets out in the three-foot aisle between the bunks. There was just room for Jack Lee to squeeze in between the stove and the door. This was the only floor space left for Jack, and it was bad luck for him.

It was a weird and spooky night. The noise of the moose blood dripping onto the tarp covering Jack's blankets didn't add much to the serenity of the close darkness, nor did the sickly smell of moose grease that permeated the atmosphere. Every little while dirt spattered down from the pole-and-dirt roof onto some object in the cabin to break the monotony of the drip drip drip of the moose blood.

Comstock had to sneak outside the cabin some time before midnight. He stepped on Jack Lee's hand on the way to the door. Jack let out a yelp.

"Sorry," Uncle Bill grunted. "Sorry, Jack. Nature's calling me."

I think everybody was awakened. Uncle Bill had hardly settled down in the blankets, having sat on my head during the process, when I heard him groan, then roll over. The house was silent once again. Then I could hear Uncle Bill muttering to himself.

"Got to go again—dammit."

I got roughed up again and my blankets pulled off as he got to his feet and made for the door. A minute later there was a muffled squawk from Jack, and I could hear Comstock floundering around trying to get his balance and find the door handle.

"What the hell goes on here anyway?" exclaimed Jack. "Ouch—you're standing on my hand again."

I could hear Uncle Bill.

"Sorry, Jack—real sorry. But I can't help it. Don't know what's gone wrong with me."

The door opened. Uncle Bill stepped out. The door closed and I dozed off.

The next thing I knew Uncle Bill was crashing around in the dark trying to get back into his bedroll. I got a knee in my face and completely lost my share of the covers.

I don't know how much later it was when I was awakened by a loud crashing noise down by Jack Lee's bed. I felt Bill's side of the bed. He was not there. He was trying to get over the top of Jack Lee's prostrate figure to reach the door. Uncle Bill was saying,

"Sorry, Jack, sorry, Jack. Can't be helped. Damn sorry, old boy—but I stepped clear of you that time."

Jack was sputtering with wrath.

"The hell you did, you big scissorbill, you stepped on my bum leg and my hand both."

Now the whole cabin was stirring with life. I guess everyone was awake. I could hear Gloria and Gertie giggling.

Some time later Uncle Bill made his fourth and last expedition across Jack Lee to the cabin door. Utter confusion, crashings and bangings ensued and Bill was saying, "Sorry, Jack, sorry, old boy."

Jack's loud whisper rang through the room.

"I sure ain't sleeping in the same house with you again, Bill. You've been steppin' on me all night. I never got no sleep and you've stove me all up. All my sore places."

This time Uncle Bill spilled snow all over my head when he got back under the covers.

"Snowing to beat hell," he whispered, "and turning real cold."

Long before daylight I was awakened by the storm. The wind whistled and howled, the cattle taking shelter around the house bawled and shoved against the walls till I thought the flimsy little building would be pushed over.

I realized that if we didn't reach Pan Meadow this day we would probably be snowed out and might not make it in there again all winter. I woke the sleepy group around the cabin. Gertie lit the fire and put the coffeepot on, while Jack Lee struggled wearily out of his sleeping bag and out into the storm to harness and take care of the team.

It was still dark when we slugged the team out onto the deep untraveled snow trail that led some twenty miles or more to the Pan Meadow.

Gloria wrapped blankets around herself and I threw a forkful of hay over the top of her. The wind swished and swirled great blinding clouds of powdery snow along our back trail. If the wind had been against us instead of at our rear the team could never have lugged us towards the Pan Meadow.

Comstock and I soon crawled into the hay beside Gloria. Jack with a blanket over his back and shoulders drove the team on towards the Blackwater Crossing and the Pan Meadow. Our wagon-box thermometer read ten below zero but we were all fairly warm and comfortable.

Ahead of us lonely mountains, canyons, rivers and swamps held only one white habitation within its boundaries, the Home Ranch, eighty miles beyond us. On a few tree-lined meadows and lakes, traveling Indian families occasionally squatted for a few weeks in the summer to fish and hunt and pick berries. The Blackwater River was an extremely dangerous barrier that split the long valley in two.

Tonight we would cross the river on the ice, then climb a thousand feet or more up the side of a heavily timbered mountain to reach Pan Meadow.

As night and the temperature closed in on us we were all conscious of a distant low rumbling sound.

"That noise," asked Gloria. "What's that?"

"Rapids below the crossing," Uncle Bill said. He cracked off the icicles on his beard, slid a pillbox around in his hand, then popped two fingers of snoose into his mouth.

"Haven't been over the crossing for twenty years," he drawled. "This could be the last time the way it sounds."

I dropped off the sleigh box and lit on top of the silent plodding Bear. His tail made two additional swings, and he fell back. The roar of the Blackwater rapids grew louder.

I floundered around in the sleigh tracks to warm up, then relieved Jack at the lines. Mike and Bud were not too happy as we approached the crossing. Their ears stood straight up, then bent forward. They brought the sleigh to a sudden stop on the low bank of the river.

The crossing looked as if it were frozen solid. The snow and wind had stopped, and by the feel of the air I knew the mercury was plunging downwards, and fast. A hundred yards or so below the approach, I could see the water boiling up from under the ice. It surged up in a mighty spray at the beginning of the rapids.

Jack Lee pulled an axe out of the sleigh box and Uncle Bill crawled down out of the hay. Nice new fresh icicles hung from his goatee, replacing the ones he had recently broken off.

"You better let me handle that axe, Jack," he whined. "You dried-out prairie men don't know water and you ain't never seen ice."

Jack was cold and he was still smarting from Uncle Bill's footwork of the night before. He handed Bill the axe without comment.

Gloria slid out from under the hay and stood on the ice at the edge of the crossing.

"What's going on now?" she said.

"We've got to test the ice," I answered.

Comstock zigzagged here and there across the ice, smashing the axe into the crust. Jack Lee had succeeded in his search for the second axe. He was using his own methods in probing the ice depths. I could see that he didn't trust Comstock's research, but I did—for Uncle Bill was a wily old lake-and-river man.

The Bear followed the two men about the ice with a dubious look on his face. Gloria walked out on her own private investigation, then walked hurriedly back to the sleigh.

"That ice can't be over three inches thick where the men are now. Every time Jack hits the ice water bubbles up. I don't want to lose my new husband over a bunch of machinery and old iron. It's not safe, Rich—anybody can see that. I'm going to put my foot down right now." She looked up at me. "We can turn around and head back for Batnuni. To heck with the Cattle Company. They can just leave their machinery there on that old meadow."

I grinned at her.

Across the river Uncle Bill and Jack and the Bear were still testing.

Gloria spoke up again. "It's not safe, Rich—you can tell just by looking at it."

"Maybe not," I said. "Depends on the ice. When the boys get back here with their measurements, then I'll know."

Gloria looked very unhappy.

Comstock had crossed back to our side of the river. He came up panting and breathing hard to the side of the team. He gave old Bud an affectionate pat on his shoulder as he went by.

"O.K.," snapped Uncle Bill. "It's O.K. You can make it. The ice is solid and rubbery, not brittle, but you'll have to cross it on the run. Three inches out there in the middle."

"O.K.," I barked at Gloria, "ask Uncle Bill about ice. He's been slicking across rivers and lakes up here for thirty years."

"What's the argument?" whined old Bill.

"Ice," Gloria said. "How much weight will it hold?"

Uncle Bill didn't look down at the ice. He'd tested that. But his long-bearded gaze went up into the darkening sky.

"Waal now, Gloria," he whined. "That's sure a mighty big question. There's all kinds of ice—brittle ice—old ice—new ice—lake ice—river ice. There's temperatures to be considered. Is it colding up or is it warming up?

"Look at that smart aleck Jack Lee. He's got it all figured out—and he don't know a damn thing about ice. Hell—he comes from Alberta."

Uncle Bill looked out towards Jack and the Bear who were now headed in our direction. I could see that neither of them looked very happy. Bill glanced at the wagon-box thermometer.

"Twenty below zero," he said. "Before that big-headed cowboy gets here I'll say this. Three inches of rubbery river ice when the weather is colding up can hold a team and load if they're moving fast. Twelve inches of black lake ice after a long cold snap can hold up a locomotive. A foot and a half of that same ice will hold up a whole freight train.

"We've got three inches of rubbery river ice in the middle of the crik. Hit her, Rich," he yelled, "and run right over the top of that Alberta cow bragger."

"Stand back," I yelled at Gloria. "Here we go."

Mike and Bud knew exactly what to do. They had been through this before. Several years ago the ice had caved in just as the team hit shore but they had been going so fast that their momentum carried us safely up on the bank as the sleigh sank into the water. I remembered looking back over the sleigh tracks and the open water that yawned up in our four-foot wake. If the team had walked or trotted we would have all been dead ducks, but they had crossed at a hard run. If we broke through this ice and dropped into the rapids beneath it I knew it would be curtains. A creepy empty feeling reached up out of the pit of my stomach.

Now the two wise old horses knew what was up. Shoulder muscles bunched up, necks reached out, nostrils expanded.

"Now boys," I said, low and easy. I shook out the lines and slowly tightened up on them. "Hit her!"

A feeling of exhilaration swept through me.

The big team sprang into their traces and we hit the ice as if we had been shot from a cannon. I could hear Bill and Jack yelling. The rubbery ice made a great bend over the main channel and it felt as if we went down many feet. For a moment I thought we were gone but then we were on the opposite bank.

When the nervous, cold, but now happy little group reached the sleigh I couldn't help breaking into a laugh.

"Bill," I yelled at the old cowman. "You're not satisfied tromping over poor old Jack all night, crippling him up, standing on his bum hand, falling over his sore knee, keeping him awake. Now you've got to rub it in on him just because he happens to hail from Alberta."

A great many Alberta cowboys are so proud of their home province that they wear you down with endless descriptions of the lush prairie wool, the beautiful scenery, the magnificent cattle, the hot chinook winds, the early springs, the clear skies and the world's champion riders. But Jack Lee was just the opposite. He talked very little. He did a lot of thinking. Jack was twenty-eight years old and a top hand.

He was just about the easiest guy to get along with that you would find in any bunkhouse between Alberta and British Columbia, but now I sensed he was tired physically and quite fed up with Uncle Bill, and I knew the feeling, for there had been times when I was ready to bust the old man over the pate with a stick of stove wood myself.

Knowing Uncle Bill better than Jack did, I could also see certain symptoms developing in the old man. Bill was tired out, cold, his bones ached. It would be only a matter of time before he would lapse into a silent meditative period that could last several days. Gloria's presence now came to our aid. With a woman on hand, even Bill's sulks would be unlikely to result in Jack's crawling a horse and riding out on us, a predicament that would be a catastrophe for the Frontier Cattle Company.

Mike and Bud were heaving and pulling against the lines. They knew that feed, water and rest were waiting for them a few miles away. I yelled at the group to stop yakking and crawl up onto the sleigh. Once more our outfit was mobile.

An hour later the big team lugged the empty sleigh up the last incline out of the Blackwater River valley.

Fine hard-driven snow hit us suddenly again. The temperature was about twenty-five below zero. We were back into the blizzard.

The interior of British Columbia is unique in this sort of sudden surprise. Fifteen hundred feet of elevation can mean the difference between calm and violence. I remember the Sierras and the San Jacintos of California where the first two thousand feet of a mountain range don't vary too much in climate. Wyoming and Colorado are much the same. But here in this part of British Columbia, what with distance north, the fairly close proximity to the sea, a wild broken-up land where mountains rise ten thousand feet straight up out of the sea—anything can happen as regards the weather.

Wind roared through the jackpines, sweeping great white gusts of powdery snow before it. The thermometer kept creeping downwards towards the thirty-below-zero mark.

There was a mile and a half of dense timber between our sleigh and the Pan Meadow cabin and it was ticklish work following the blazes on the seldom-used trail through the heavy growth of jackpine.

I was worried about Gloria and concerned about old Bill.

We buried Gloria in hay and blankets. Uncle Bill picked up the lines while Jack and I floundered through the trees feeling for old blazes.

Mike and Bud finally lugged the sleigh onto the big opening. The deserted, gloomy-looking log house faced us in all its haunted glory.

The door was locked. I grabbed out an axe and broke the hinges loose. Jack led the team down a little hill to the barn. Comstock found candles and started a fire in the cookstove.

The air was heavy with the rank smell of pack rats. Nine or ten piles of rubbish spread across the room. It was alive with the rats. With a shovel and some spruce boughs for brooms we managed to clean out enough floor space to roll out our beds.

"Is anyone going to use this table for anything?" Uncle Bill wanted to know. "Waal, I'm putting my blanket right up here on top of it. Those pack rats are not going to run all over my beard down there on the floor tonight."

Our food had practically run out. Gertie Hill had generously offered us a big chunk of moose meat, but in our hurry to hit the trail we had forgotten it.

Gloria fried up two slices of bacon for each of us and a kettle of rice. Uncle Bill stirred up some brown, rather lumpy, frying-pan gravy. We ate what there was.

The only space that wasn't taken up with pack-rat nests was under Uncle Bill's table. Jack Lee rolled his bed out there.

At last we were all settled in our beds, Comstock, a comical-looking figure, stretched out on the dining room table, his long beard tinged with the brown stains of snoose flowing out onto his mackinaw coat, and his long-visored beagle cap pulled down over his eyes.

Someone blew out the candle and the rats came out by the dozen. Gloria put her head under the tarp and the blankets. Rats, big heavy fellows, darted here and there across our tarp bed covering. The Bear chased them around the cabin. Outside the wind wailed and moaned through the jackpines and fine gusts of snow sifted through the open cracks between the logs.

Uncle Bill left the cabin only once during the night. He stepped on Jack Lee's bum leg. Jack yelled. Comstock said,

"Sorry, Jack. Sorry, old boy. Couldn't see you there in the dark. You're right under my bed you know."

The following dawn broke clear and icy cold. Thermometer registered forty-two below zero.

Jack and I assembled machinery and tools at the sleigh. We took off the poles and loaded up two big heavy-duty Massey-Harris oil-bath mowers and a rake. It was cold miserable work, and it was dark by the time the sleigh was loaded.

During the day Gloria admitted that she had been having pains in her appendix. Apparently it had been bothering her off and on for a couple of weeks but she hadn't wanted to mention it and worry us.

My God, I thought. If she gets an appendix attack here—she's had it! It would take at least seven days by sleigh traveling around the clock through the deep snow to get her out to a doctor.

I made up my mind then and there that if we got out of this trap safely I was going to make plans to move somewhere closer to civilization—and just as soon as it was humanly possible.

Gloria groaned and rolled about during the night. For breakfast Uncle Bill, Jack Lee, the Bear and I finished the last of our grub, one hotcake apiece, and then closed the door on the pack rats, leaving them in peace and to their own devices.

It was a long, miserable, bone-chilling day. The snow was deep and the load was a heavy one. It was just too much to expect Mike and Bud to lug twenty miles in one day.

Gloria was as white as the snow around her, and very quiet.

Fortunately for us the intense cold had tightened up the Blackwater and we crossed without incident.

A short time before dark Jack let the team stop for a breather. We fed them the last of the hay.

"I'll tell you buckaroos what we're going to do right now," Comstock barked. "We're going to unload the machinery and burn a rag into Hills'."

"Only sensible thing," Jack Lee agreed. "If Gloria's appendix gets any worse we can move straight on to Batnuni with an empty sleigh, change horses and slug on to Vanderhoof."

"Let's get her unloaded," I said.

It was nearly midnight with the mercury at the thirty-below-zero mark when the team swung off the road onto the Hill meadow.

I was surprised to see a faint light showing through the cracks of the Hills' door. Fresh sleigh tracks gleamed up in the moonlight.

Jack Lee drove the team to the cabin. Comstock crawled stiffly down from the load. He helped Gloria to the doorway. One of her cheeks was frosted.

The door of the cabin flew open and Johnny Slash, an Indian friend of mine from Trout Lake village, stepped outside.

"Mrs. Hill died last night. Some kind of heart. Gertie she ride saddle horse all the way to Nazko to get me— then all the way back. Mr. Hill inside too. All kinds people stop that cabin."

Mr. Hill stuck his head out of the door.

"Come in, folks," he called. "Come in out of the cold."

Jack and I led the team to the stackyard where the cattle were bawling and milling about.

"That's sure tough," Jack said. "Sure tough on Gertie."

"I wonder where they put Mrs. Hill's body. Thirty below is a hell of a time to die. There sure ain't enough room in the cabin for all that mob and Mrs. Hill too."

Jack and I entered the cabin and a curtain of blue steam came in with us. I saw a mop of black hair sticking out from under the blankets in one bed.

I looked at Jack. His jaw was sagging.

Gertie and her father were taking the blow like the real frontier people they were, both calm and neither of them forgetting their usual hospitality. Gloria slumped down on one bed and as the cold worked out of her she shook violently.

I saw the head of black hair under the blankets start to move and I just about took off. Then Mrs. Johnny Slash rose up on her elbows.

Gertie poured us hot coffee and sliced fresh bread. We thawed Gloria out. Gertie put moose steaks on the stove.

Some time after two A.M. Gloria and I dug a hole in the haystack and rolled up in our sleeping bags. My exhausted bride slept better than I did.

At daylight we loaded Mrs. Hill's body on a sleigh. She had been rolled up in a tarp and buried in the hay, not far from where Gloria and I slept. During the night cattle broke into the stackyard and ate the hay from around the tarp.

It was decided that our party would stay at Hills' feeding the cattle and horses. The Hill family and the Indians would travel to Nazko Indian village where help could be gathered and Mrs. Hill could be given a decent burial, with some kind of a service.

We also decided that if Gloria had another appendix attack, I would rush her out to Batnuni, change to a four-up, and pound into Vanderhoof while Jack stayed on and fed the cattle until Gertie and her father arrived back from Nazko.

The Slashes and Mr. Hill got under way with their two sleighs and Gertie, true to form, hit the trail on a saddle horse. I knew she would ride into the Indian village hours ahead of Slash and Hill, that the grave-digging with axes, spades and crowbars through five feet of frozen ground would be well under way when the sleighs arrived.

We stayed at Hills' meadow for four days until Gertie and old Mr. Hill returned, during which time we went back after the machinery. Mr. Hill was close to seventy at the time and in very poor health. He was unable to do any physical work at all. Gertie would have to perform a man's work now.

She had seventy head of cattle to pitch hay to, dragging the hay out of ice-caked stacks, watering the stock by axing large holes in the ice. She would have to haul in wood and saw it by hand for the stove, shoot and butcher moose for food.

When Gertie returned, Comstock and I told her there was just one thing for her to do. Have Johnny Slash and the Indians drive her stock out to Nazko and sell the works. She would sell at a loss but at least she would come out of the deal with some money and her life and health intact.

But Gertie was stubborn.

"I'm staying with it," she said. And she did.

Today Gertie is happily married and lives out in civilization in a modern house with her several children, a big change in environment from the remote hay camp on Poplar Mountain.

CHAPTER IV

Batnuni Underworld

WHEN WE FINALLY ARRIVED at Batnuni Lake the machinery-salvaging trip to Pan Meadow had absorbed fifteen days instead of the estimated eight.

"Whoa, boys," Jack Lee yelled to the team as we drew abreast of Uncle Bill's cabin.

"You folks are my guests for luncheon," drawled Uncle Bill. He helped Gloria off the pile of rake teeth and mowing machines and parts.

It was a clear sunshiny day, and so warm that I had stripped to the waist hoping to pick up a bit of suntan.

I cut a hole in the ice to water the team, Jack gave the horses a forkful of hay, and we followed Uncle Bill's large tracks and Gloria's smaller ones up the short incline to the cabin.

The shack was like an icebox. We found Gloria standing by the cold stove, her eyes wide. Uncle Bill was sweeping bucketfuls of ice and frozen beer slush off the floor.

"Too bad," exclaimed Jack Lee. "The end of Bill's beer and the end of the party!"

I looked around the once-immaculate room. It presented an extraordinary sight.

Ketchup bottles, beer bottles, wine bottles, vinegar bottles, and an assortment of condiments had frozen in such a manner that the various liquids had lifted off lids and tops. The iced ingredients had risen gradually towards the ceiling, carrying the bottle tops perched like hats on their heads.

Gloria could not understand the enormous gallonage of frozen beer. What had the abstemious Uncle Bill intended to do with at least two dozen cases of beer that had blown up in their hiding places, under his bed, in the cupboard, and in the bottom of his clothes closet? What she didn't know, was that there were another ten dozen cases of beer, not frozen, but cached safely away down in a dirt cellar beneath the floor of the cabin, reached only by a ladder beneath a hidden trap door in one corner of the room.

I had not yet got around to describing to Gloria my underworld activities in Batnuni Valley, my official position as first vice-president, treasurer and director of the exclusive Batnuni Valley Range Exploration and Drinking Club. I had been reticent about letting Gloria in on the history and the black secrets of this organization, and so had the other members of the Batnuni Valley Range Exploration and Drinking Club who were in the country at the time.

The history of the club and the reason for Bill's large stock of homemade beer went back some years.

Out of Batnuni's isolation from the social activities of the outside world arose a serious problem. In the development days the hired hands wanted to get outside occasionally and associate with people other than ourselves. Often it would be four or five months before the boys could leave the ranch for their well-earned vacations. Usually I arranged for two or three of the men to ride to town together.

Allowing about six days' traveling time, depending on the condition of the trail and of the horses they rode, plus four or five days in town, they would be expected back in two weeks. Usually a shaky, irritable and sad-faced group of ranch hands crawled down from tired horses two days to two weeks late.

Human nature is human nature even on the remote ranges of British Columbia and there isn't much you can do about it. However, Uncle Bill finally figured out a way to make the boys love the good old Batnuni. He could produce a super home brew out of malt, hops, sugar and a few raisins.

"The boys will never want to leave home once they try this nourishing refreshment," he told me.

It was agreed that the Frontier Company would get a license from the Royal Canadian Mounted Police and furnish the ingredients and the barrels and bottles. Bill agreed to make and keep on hand two forty-five-gallon barrels of beer. We would keep the plan strictly hush-hush until the beer was well aged and ready for consumption. In the backlands, very few brews were ever allowed to survive the green bubbling or mash stage. The results were always the same. Intoxicated or not, the imbibers always ended the supposedly happy hours desperately ill, and for several days thereafter would be unfit for any kind of work.

Bill and I drew up the rules and regulations of a super men's club. Beer was served in the summer out on the lawn overlooking Batnuni Lake. A large barrel sat firmly upon a heavy axe-hewed plank stand.

Large tin mugs that could hold twelve ounces of beer as well as the foam, were lined up on a second table. There were no chairs or stools in evidence. Bill charged ten cents a mug for beer. The boys who never carried change or bills in their pockets—because they were always broke to start with—signed chits.

I subtracted their total chits from their wage account with the Company, and once a month wrote a check to Bill who, in turn, subtracted the initial Company investment in beer and equipment from his profits.

No one was allowed to sit down or lie down on the club premises, but as long as we held our feet under us, did not become sick, abusive or unable to crawl up on our saddle horses to ride home to the ranch, club members were allowed to drink all they wished.

Anyone breaking any of the Range Exploration and Drinking Club rules was suspended from the club for an indefinite period of time.

Newly arrived ranch hands were never told of the existence of the club, and were not asked to join unless they had toughed out at least one month on the Batnuni range.

The Range Exploration and Drinking Club turned out to be a real morale raiser. Week-end evenings were looked forward to with great anticipation, and a world of fun and joking about the various club activities, its rules, its exclusive patronage and many other aspects, tickled the humor of the cowboys.

Once every month there was a ladies' night. Lucille Dwinnell was usually our one lady guest. At such festive occasions we were all allowed to sit down on the lawn and every member was on his very best behavior.

Trips to town became fewer and farther apart, and Uncle Bill's beer left few hangovers. The boys had a kind of unwritten law among themselves that the week-end celebrations should not affect their work or responsibilities.

Often I wished that one of us had owned a camera and been able to take pictures of some of the club gatherings. Sometimes on Saturday nights there would be six or eight saddle horses tied to Uncle Bill's hitch rail and a wagon or two, horses grazing along the lake shore. Possibly there would be the addition of a hay rake, a stacker and mowing machine when hay season was on and we were moving a haying outfit to a wild meadow.

Among wagons, machinery and horses, there would be the chap-clad, moose-hided figures of many darkly tanned men, sometimes a trusted Indian or two, all holding giant mugs, and Uncle Bill's long-bearded presence at the spigot of the beer barrel.

Uncle Bill wasn't very happy about his burst bottles of beer, and neither was Jack or I.

"There's no use me carrying on here," he whined. "I might as well go on with you folks to the ranch. Then I can keep an eye on Jack here and Harold, while Rich whips Gloria into Vanderhoof to see a doctor about her appendix."

"Bring along a case of beer from you know where," I told him.

I could see Jack Lee wasn't very happy about being Uncle Bill's future roommate, but he grinned widely.

"That's just fine," Jack said. "Bill will be upstairs in the bunkhouse room, and every time he wants to go outside, there'll be nobody to tromp on. There'll just be those stairs. Straight up and down like a ladder. If he ever gets balled up and misses a step, and I'll bet he will, he'll cripple hisself instead of tromping all over somebody else."

We slid into the ranch just in time. Harold Dwinnell was preparing to ride out that night on our tracks to find out what had happened to us.

After a day's rest, Gloria and I jumped our two saddle horses and, leading two pack horses, headed for Vanderhoof.

The ranch gang and the Dwinnell children stood in a body around the white-bearded Comstock as we rode off, and the last thing I heard was Uncle Bill's command to Jack Lee,

"As long as I'm takin' charge around here, I'm going to see Lucille gets stove wood. Down with you, Jack, to the woodpile with an axe and fill up that woodbox. What you doing up here actin' like a social man when there's work to be done?"

This was a tough trip for Gloria. A heavy crust had formed on the three feet of snow on the mountains. The saddle horses would be thrown off balance and flounder about in their tracks. Many times during each day we had to crawl down and lead the horses.

Gloria, who brought up the rear, had to pick her feet up high and step far ahead to stay in the horse tracks. She developed a bad case of what we call snowshoe cramp, a form of strain in the upper leg muscles. However, we made it through to Elijah Hargreaves' in four long days. Elijah had traded a cow for an old wreck of a car. I think this stylish vehicle was a 1924 Buick. He managed to get the engine started and insisted on driving us the rest of the way to town.

The doctor diagnosed Gloria's appendix trouble as chronic and said there was little danger of its rupturing. She was allowed to go back to the ranch, but we made arrangements to have her appendix removed later on.

CHAPTER V

We Buy a Ranch

CANADA'S BEEF MARKET was tied to Britain on contract all through the war years and an embargo on shipments to other countries including the United States was rigidly enforced. While ranchers in the States were receiving excellent prices for their beef, their Canadian neighbors went broke by the thousands. Wages, scarcity of labor and high prices for practically everything but beef caused a great hardship on those individuals who worked twelve to sixteen hours a day at one of the toughest businesses that exists.

This same condition plagued the Canadian ranges until the end of 1948 when the embargo to the States was lifted. Canadian beef prices for good Hereford yearlings off grass seldom went higher than six and a half to seven and a half cents on the hoof, while the Chicago and Omaha markets were paying up to twenty-four cents for the same class of beef.

With the cutback of breeding stock on the Frontier Cattle Company ranches it was obvious after two years' reduced operation that the project could not carry on and pay wages. Harold Dwinnell and Jack Lee, after a monumental amount of brainwork, devised a plan that looked good to me. They were prepared to lease the Batnuni, Pan Meadow, McNutt place and Pennoyer Meadow on a fifty-fifty calf-share split. The lease would run for three years. At the end of three years Dwinnell and Lee would turn back to the Company the total number of cows that they had originally leased. Losses were to be replaced out of their share of heifer calves and yearlings. They were to have the use of the Company horses and all equipment, drive to market each year their own as well as the Company's half share of the yearly beef.

I knew this was a big break for the Frontier Company as the Batnuni herd was gradually being depleted to pay off expenses. And this fitted in well with my plans since Gloria and I wanted a ranch of our own.

I had a hunch where our future spread would be. Several years before Gloria and I were married I had flown into the Home Ranch with our Company bookkeeper and secretary, Judge Stephen Holmes, of Vanderhoof. Some thirty air miles southwest of Vanderhoof our plane circled a lush green valley with a small lake at its lower end and a winding willow-bottom creek twisting for miles through its center. From the air I could see several old fallen-in corrals and dilapidated buildings and noted that there were hundreds of acres of willow bottom, the best potential hay land of the north country. A high craterlike volcanic rimrock mountain walled the valley off from the dark spruce and pine jungles that stretched north almost to Vanderhoof. Judge Holmes thought that the main part of this deserted valley was owned by the Dahl family.

While Gloria and I were in town seeing about her appendix, we looked up Earl Dahl, who owned the one taxi in Vanderhoof. He went over various maps with me and we both came to the conclusion that it was his family's old ranch that I had seen from the air. Earl's father had passed away a number of years before and Earl and his mother had the ranch up for sale. Earl volunteered to drive us over the back bush road to look at the property, and armed with chains, shovels and axes and a home-made winch, Earl, Mrs. Dahl, Gloria and I and the old Bear struck out for the rimrock valley.

Several hours of snow shoveling and winching over bad spots saw us through to the gap in the rimrock mountain. Here the country made a sudden and breath-taking change. We dropped down into the deep valley basin. Partly open hills sloped off the steep rimrock and ended at a long sweep of open meadow and willow clumps bisected by a clear sand-bottom creek. Far down the opening we could see the octopus-shaped lake. It was warm down in the valley. The snow was thawing fast. Part of the meadow was already bare and I could see patches of open water in the distant lake.

I found two small creeks that flowed into the lake. A four-foot beaver dam held back the water. I saw at once that a large acreage of first-class bottomland was under water. It would be easy to knock out the dam, drain the meadow and install a log headgate to regulate the water in the future.

This looked like a wonderful layout to me and although I saw Gloria dubiously eying the discouraged-looking buildings sticking up out of the snowdrifts she raised no objections when I shook hands with Earl and Mrs. Dahl and we headed for town to have the papers drawn up for the transfer of the property to us.

It was green-grass time at Batnuni. The snow had melted. The ground gave off that rank earthy smell of last fall's rotting leaves and decayed vegetation, the clean new aroma of young grass, and willow buds and poplar sprouts. The faint smell of the evergreen pine mingled with all the other wonderful smells of spring. The sun was glaring hot and a faint breeze blew out of the west. The long hard winter was over, and now all of nature's wondrous live things were coming forth into new life. The air was filled with bird song, squirrel chatter and all manner of happy sounds.

Gloria and I decided to take a wagonload of our belongings to our new Rimrock Ranch. As Harold had to make a trip to town to sign the lease papers and line up his summer supplies for Batnuni, he decided to come along with us. Harold drove the loaded wagon with Mike and Bud in the traces and Gloria and I rode Stuyve and Rhino and led Nimpo.

Bill Comstock had left the ranch for his trap cabin some time before. It seems that he had begun to order Lucille about the house, and had criticized her biscuits. After a bit of this, Lucille had told him in a quiet polite way that, after all, he was at the ranch as a guest, not as a general supervisor of the kitchen. The boys were gone during the day, and old Bill's main pastime was nipped in the bud.

He slung his pack board on his back and struck out in long jerky strides for his cabin and his trap line.

Harold got a big laugh out of the whole thing.

"I'm the only person gets along with the old fellow. That's because I know how to handle him."

Jack Lee snorted and said nothing.

Lucille turned from her bread baking.

"You'll find out, Harold, how well you can get along with old Uncle Bill if you ever have to have him around you all day, day after day, with no end in sight."

As our safari approached Bill's cabin, Harold pulled up the team, and I reined in Rhino, and the bearded old giant stepped through the cabin door. He bowed to Gloria, passed the usual polite words of greeting, then whined at Harold and me.

"Where you takin' the charming young lady today?"

"We're on our way to our new ranch," Gloria said.

"Waal now," whined old Bill, "I might as well go along with you folks. Unless I come along, Gloria will have no one with any intelligence to talk to on that long trip. You two knotheads haven't got the brains or the proper education to talk about anything but cows and horses. I want to see that ranch of Gloria's anyway."

"Come on with us, Uncle Bill," Gloria said, "and bring some more books."

Harold and I grinned at the old man, and I barked at him to make it snappy and throw his soogans and rags in the wagon box.

"We ain't got all day," Harold snapped.

And so we rode and rolled out of Batnuni Valley with Uncle Bill once more on the load, the self-appointed boss, manager and supervisor of the expedition.

It was a good trip. The spring mud up in the mountains

was the only drawback. It was hard on horses. We made Marvin Lake that first night, some sixteen miles, and turned the five horses loose in the one-acre log-fenced holding pasture, where three inches of new green grass formed a thick carpet above the half-thawed ground. We threw the horses hay and grained the team.

Uncle Bill started his drawling whine at Harold to bring ropes and axe and go with him to the lake.

"If the ice is gone, you're gonna build a raft, and I'll show you how to do it. Then I'll show you where we can catch a mess of rainbows for supper."

Gloria started lining up the supper materials, pots and pans, knives and forks, bread, cooked beans and chicken noodle soup, on a four-foot-square piece of oilcloth, which she laid out by the fire.

This oilcloth idea, in place of a dirty old tarp, saddle blanket, or a pair of chaps for a tablecloth was her own invention, and she was extremely proud of it. Gloria gave the red and white oilcloth a couple of pats with her hand, cocked her head to one side, surveyed her work, her long blond hair falling over one shoulder.

She looked up at us.

"Look, boys, isn't this nice? Aren't you all lucky to have a nice clean table to eat on instead of your old saddle blankets?"

"Beautiful, Gloria," Bill said, admiration showing all over his face. "It's sure plumb beautiful. Been freighting in the mountains forty years and never thought of it myself. Now, Harold, get going with that axe and rope for a dry tree on the lake shore, and you, Rich, get busy and bring in the night's wood and set up the tents. I'm

going in my duffle for my fishing tackle. Then I'll show
you young punks another lesson on how to keep from
starving to death in the woods."

Old Bill whistled through his nose, and with long
strides headed for his dufflebag and then the lake.

Harold didn't have to build a raft as ten feet of open
water separated the shore and the ice.

Strangely enough, Bill and Harold arrived back in
camp with eight or ten magnificently colored red and
purple rainbows, weighing between one and two
pounds each.

I couldn't believe my eyes.

"Unbelievable," I sputtered.

"Good for you, Uncle Bill." Gloria smiled admiringly.
"I just knew you'd do it."

"I just showed Harold where to put that line in the
water between shore and ice under a rock ledge, but
the boy got careless and fell in."

I looked at Harold. He was wet to the waist and was
glaring at Uncle Bill.

"That's what Bill says," snapped Harold. "He showed
me a piece of rotten ice to stand on, said there was land
underneath it. There was, under three feet of water.
Should have used my own judgment instead of listening
to that long-bearded old banshee."

Gloria jumped up from the cook fire that crackled and
blazed up into the evening dusk.

"Have you got a towel and a change, Harold?" she
said. "If not, Rich can lend you some of his clothes, and
I've got a towel."

"Thanks, Gloria." Harold smiled. "For once I've got

everything I need in the wagon. Lucille packed up all my duds."

From Batnuni to our Rimrock Ranch was an estimated distance of some hundred miles. We made the trip in eight days. At one particular stretch, on a high plateau, the frost was going out of the ground, and we were lucky to make four miles in one day. In places the wagon sank to the wheel hubs. Another day under the same conditions, Mike and Bud went their heavy-bodied, strong-hearted limit to move the outfit five miles.

On several long stretches of almost bottomless muck, Uncle Bill took over the lines while Harold and I tied onto the wagon tongue with our lariats. Both Nimpo and Rhino were used to mud, to ropes, and they were not afraid to get in there with everything they had on a long hard pull.

Harold and I took the kinks out of our ropes as our saddle horses lugged and splashed and plowed ahead of the team. With the four horses, we got the wagon through. I was thankful that Uncle Bill was with us, for Gloria could never have handled the team through the mud.

We held a conference with the Goodlands. It was decided that they would join us for a month at Rimrock, put the buildings in order, and build a new log cabin. Jean and Sam would bring in their wagon with all sorts of tools, house jacks and other gadgets which we didn't possess.

At last the deep gap in the forest loomed ahead of us. One minute you could see the high timbered hills on both sides, the flat spruce jungle reaching ahead, and then suddenly you were dropping down into the extinct

volcano with its open grassy hills streaking high into the
sky towards the towering black rimrock.

Down, down, down, the wagon rolled. The brakes skidded and wheels squealed, and the team dug in their front
feet, and hunched back against the neck yoke, their hind
feet squarely under them. The wide green meadow, the lake
in the distance, the winding willow-bottom creek, were
coming up fast.

"The damn brake lining's out again," yelled Harold.

Now the wagon was on the bottom. The ranch
buildings lay a quarter of a mile ahead. I left the crashing and banging iron-wheeled wagon behind me and
trotted on ahead.

The snow had long since melted, and all that had lain
beneath the clean white mantle was exposed to view. The
deserted buildings loomed up ugly, dirty and unkempt.

Dozens of old half-rotten sheep hides were scattered
about between piles of rubbish and rusted tin cans.
Several disintegrated bodies of long-dead Hereford cattle
lay in a heap in a ditch, almost directly in front of the
main ranchhouse. Around them were the skulls and bones
and parts of the hides of more sheep.

The ditches and low spots in front of the workshop
and barn were bulging with large piles of driftwood roots
and other interesting concentrations. In fact most of the
open space around the buildings was loaded. An old
chicken house directly in front of the workshop had
caved in on one side, and the frost had reared up the
other, so that boards and nails popped up where the roof
had been.

It was some sight, but I knew the answers. The ranch

buildings had been left on their own, years before, when the Dahls had moved out to town. Naturally they were not in good repair. A flood two years before had lifted the tincan and garbage dump from its moorings, some distance above the buildings, and scattered the works in a thorough manner in the front yard.

The sheep hides, which weren't worth the money to freight to town, had floated on down with the garbage and cans. A few of the Dahls' cattle and sheep which they had been unable to locate when they shipped for the last time, had come down out of the hills and dug into a trough of lime mix with which the family were going to work over the buildings.

I knew all this because Mrs. Dahl had told me about it, but Gloria knew nothing about the whole thing. I hadn't dared tell her about the mess. My bride had been a bit squeamish regarding the proposition as it was.

Now as the bang and crash of the iron-wheeled wagon sounded nearer and nearer, then suddenly flashed into view around a clump of diamond willows, my legs began quaking against my chaps.

Boy, oh boy, I thought, I'll catch hell when Gloria sees all this.

A heavy-duty log bridge spanned the gravel-bottomed creek in front of the house. I could see green grass on the far bank.

I'll leave those people to explain and let Gloria blow her top while I take care of the saddle horses.

The wagon was now drawing up through the garbage in the yard. I hurriedly led my horses across the bridge and behind some willows on the other side of the creek, out of sight of the house. There I started to unsaddle and take off my chaps. I could hear Gloria's voice above those of the men.

I got out of there just in time, I thought.

After I had unsaddled and turned the horses loose, I watched them roll, get their legs under them, heave to their feet, shake themselves and then gaze out at the great grassy meadow that reached off towards the distant pine-clad hills.

Rhino was a smart horse, he was almost human. He loved to play tricks on me and quite often when I turned him loose after a long day's ride, he would look over at me, raise a lip and blink an eye at me. He would study me for a moment, waiting for instructions, such as, "Don't pull out on me, you old hammerhead, I'm giving you a real break tonight," or in a more cranky tone, "If you leave me afoot and pull out, I'll slam on those hobbles and give you a real ride."

Then the young fellow would walk high-tonedly away switching his tail and, to test me out, keep walking through the good feed, as if he really were leaving me behind.

"Hey, you," I'd yell, "where the hell you think you're going?"

Without even glancing in my direction, and pretending he hadn't heard me at all, Rhino would down his head in the grass, and the evening's play would be over. Now the grassy prospect that reached out ahead of him stunned him for a moment, a horse heaven greater even than his wildest dreams.

Rhino swung his head towards me in mild disbelief.

"Go ahead, dig in, old snoot face." I gave him a slap

on the rump. Single file the horses walked off into the green grass and the gathering dusk.

I watched them for a moment, then walked to the bridge where Harold met me, leading Mike and Bud.

Harold looked over his shoulder. Gloria and Uncle Bill had apparently picked their way safely through the various obstructions in the front yard, and entered the ranchhouse. I could vaguely hear Uncle Bill's whining comments about something or other, and Gloria's smooth monologue, going on and on.

Harold grinned. "Boy, you've got lots of grass and side hills and meadow and water here, and that's what makes a ranch. But what a mess—the yard and buildings."

Bud pushed Harold forward with his big head. The cowboy lost his balance and almost fell into the creek. He pulled Bud's halter off, then Mike's. The team kicked high into the air and with loud snorts of joy plunged across the rest of the bridge and thundered out onto the meadow heading for Rhino, Nimpo and Stuyve.

Harold and I crossed over to the ranchhouse and walked through the door. I had seen so many of British Columbia's backwoods deserted houses that this one was no surprise to me. In one quick glance I saw the porch and the living room. Chickens had been roosting on the porch. Several old chairs and tables lay broken in half or legless about the floor, among packing boxes, a pack-rat nest or two and piles of old newspapers.

Gloria and Uncle Bill were surveying the pack-rat paradise in the living room where every conceivable kind of art treasure, including the best types of broken china, were strewn, forlorn and long neglected, about the floor.

"This is not such a bad room," Gloria was saying.

"Burn her down," Uncle Bill was repeating. "Burn the old junk heap down. That's the only way out. I've got plenty of matches in my pocket. Say the word and we'll have a real nice bonfire tonight."

"This room has big possibilities," Gloria said, staring along the walls, the floor and the ceiling. "Those two bedrooms over there can be enlarged, cupboards built, new windows. I think I'll have to paint everything white.

"Two picture windows over here on the south side of the room, overlooking that beautiful little brook and the distant blue mountains. Glass-enclosed porch running the full length of the house, on the east end of the living room, facing that lovely green meadow."

"Burn her down," whined Uncle Bill. "I've got lots of matches right here in my pocket."

Gloria suddenly noticed Harold and me standing in the living room doorway and snapped out of her interior decorator's trance.

"Look, Rich—isn't this terrific? Just think of all the things we can do with this house. Over there we can put that couch I've got in storage in Vancouver. The back porch can be made into a glass-enclosed kitchen-dining room. What wonderful possibilities!"

I looked at Harold. Both of us were in a state of shock. Instead of the screams of condemnation and wrath that we had steeled ourselves to face, we were now over-whelmed with Gloria's rapid-fire enthusiasm.

"Burn her down," whined Uncle Bill. "I like to burn old rat heaps down and build something nice and new in their place. I got lots of matches."

Gloria turned to old Comstock.

"Are you sure you've got a lot of matches, Uncle Bill?" she coyly asked.

Bill felt in his shirt pocket. He thrust out a handful of dubious-looking old matches for Gloria to see.

"Lots," he said.

"Fine," replied Gloria. "Now go out there to that old fallen-in chicken house, and set it on fire. That's a good use for those matches of yours. Next, you can set fire to that ugly pile of refuse we can see from the window here. Then Rich and Harold can start picking up and throwing all those old sheep hides and miscellaneous stuff into the flames. We'll have the worst of the eyesores around here cleaned up by dark tonight."

Uncle Bill's mouth fell wide open, and his long goatee quivered with emotion.

Harold looked at me and shook his head, a sheepish grin spread across his face. "Ya know, when I was young I thought I savvied women. When I grew up I began to wonder whether I did or not. Now I know I don't."

CHAPTER VI

The Tatuk Grizzlies

SEVERAL DAYS AFTER OUR cleaning-up spree at Rimrock, we heard the clatter and banging of an iron-wheeled wagon approaching the ranch buildings and Sam and Jean Goodland came into view riding on top of a load of tools, lumber and crates of windowglass.

It was now time for me to saddle up and ride back to Batnuni to carry out my last summer's contract with the Frontier Cattle Company. The Bear and the Queen and Gloria were to stay at Rimrock with the Goodlands and carry on with the building schedule, and Gloria's mother, whom I called Aunt Kate, was coming up from Vancouver to spend the summer. Harold and Bill Comstock had already pulled out on our wagon for town for supplies and then for Batnuni.

I reluctantly waved good-bye to the group in front of the ranchhouse and hit the trail southwards.

Two days later I was riding through the lower spruce-jungle slopes of the Tatuk Mountains when Rhino and Nimpo started prancing about and shying off to the side of the trail, doing their very best to turn about and head in the opposite direction.

Grizzly tracks were lined out in the muddy trail in the

same direction we were traveling. A faint haze hung in the mud bottom of some of the tracks. The big bear was not far in the lead.

Dusk was settling slowly down around us. Overturned roots of giant spruce, low-hanging moss on tree limbs and tree trunks, the strange shape of distorted waterlogged spruce in the gathering dark, gave me a weird and spooky feeling. This was the darkest and gloomiest stretch of country between Rimrock and Batnuni.

The horses were approaching our night camp—the lone corral on a small spruce-jungle creek—that we called Camp 44. I had often seen large grizzly tracks in this vicinity at the edge of the Tatuk Mountains.

The bear was almost certain to stop for the night somewhere in the neighborhood of 44 Creek, where I planned to book myself into camp. It was the only place for miles around us where there was horse feed, water and dry wood. The worst part of my situation was that I had left the old Bear back at Rimrock to keep guard on Gloria and Aunt Kate.

I watched every bush ahead of me and on each side of the trail. Darkness closed down around us. Rhino and Nimpo didn't snap out of their nervousness. It was not a good sign. We danced and pranced into my spruce tree camp on the banks of the creek.

While I set up camp I thought of the history of grizzly bears in the Tatuk Mountains and the Itchas.

Ever since Vanderhoof was first settled, trappers and Indians have drifted into the village with terrifying tales of the monstrous reddish-brown grizzly bears that infest the mysterious spruce jungles of the Tatuk Lake Mountains, giant bears they say, who break the backs of bull moose with a single swat of a paw, attack a man or horse on sight, and leave sixteen-inch tracks in the mud.

The few of us who live in or near the vast maze of swamps and muskegs and dense bush of this spooky grizzly country have had some mighty scary bear adventures. But bear stories are so common around here that the listener will likely fall asleep unless there's a real humdinger of a story to tell, like Joe Murray's horrifying ordeal with a band of Tatuk Lake grizzlies.

It is doubtful if any accurate analysis of the workings of a grizzly's mind has yet been set down on paper. But in order to stay out of trouble, backwoodsmen and trappers and packers of the North Country nearly all agree on certain known grizzly rules, rules that seem to prove out in about eight cases out of ten.

First, one must realize that grizzlies traveling over their own personal areas in isolated districts, where they have never come in contact with man and his firearms, are lord and master of all they survey. An old grizzly puts the run on all other animals. He is not even afraid of hungry wolf packs. Only once have I heard of a wolf pack overcoming a grizzly, and then there were over twenty wolves in the pack.

The grizzly apparently doesn't know the meaning of fear. He travels where he wishes. He is a curious animal. He will often stand on his hind legs to watch and study the strange figure of a man not too many windfalls away from him, with no intention of attacking.

Louis Kohse, who now owns Joe Murray's Tatuk Lake trap line, had a spine-tingling experience with the monstrous animals. Louis was cautiously picking his way across a wide muskeg where one misstep would plunge him to his elbows in the ooze, when he heard the swish of heavy bodies padding through the bush on the edge of the bog.

Louis told me: "I stopped walking and looked over my shoulder to see what was moving. A red bear that looked as big as an elephant ambled out on the edge of the muskeg. He was about a hundred and fifty yards from me. I looked at the .22-caliber rifle I was packing and knew the little gun was useless. I still had a quarter of a mile of open going to reach the trees. There was only one thing to do—keep walking. I stepped along real slow so I wouldn't break through the muskeg.

"The next time I looked back I was sure my day had come. There were three bears following me. One was the big boar and there were two two-year-olds. I wondered where the female was—and then I saw her, directly in my path on the far side of the muskeg. She was tearing away at a moose she'd just killed.

"I walked at an angle away from the sow which gave me another three hundred yards to cover. That was the longest short walk I ever put in in my life. The three bears came up within a hundred yards of me and kept that distance across the rest of the bog. Then they ambled off to join the she-bear and her kill. They paid no more attention to me."

Louis stutters when he gets excited. He broke into a sweat while telling me the story and ended by saying,

"Makes you stop and think when you have four of those b-b-big b-b-bastards on your b-b-b-backtrail."

Once, north of the Tatuk Mountains, I had the pleasant experience of spending the night in a pup tent within a hundred yards of a grizzly who was pulling a 1,200-pound, bogged-down cow out of a water hole up three feet onto a narrow bridge. I could hear the crunch and crackle of bones and the belching growling noises, and smell the behemoth when he came up to examine the tent. If I had shot at that bear in the dark he would have torn the mosquito tent and myself to bits.

He scared my saddle horses off during the long, long night and by morning I was gibbering like an idiot and didn't wait to cook any breakfast before hitting the trail. This bear's tracks measured fifteen inches in the mud. He carried the 1,200-pound Hereford cow across the bridge into the woods, pulled it apart and devoured nearly one hindquarter before the sun broke over the mountains. Authorities who should know believe that these giant reddish-brown bears are a cross between grizzlies and Alaska browns, the biggest bears in the world.

Here in central British Columbia men have been killed when they excitedly fired at a curious grizzly who more often than not was about to drop to all fours and amble slowly away. A startled or wounded grizzly will charge eight or nine times out of ten.

When Panhandle Phillips and I were packing supplies over the Itcha and Tatuk mountains where we encountered numerous family bands of grizzlies, we always belled several of the pack horses to warn the bears of our approach.

If you come suddenly upon a grizzly and through fright break into a run in the opposite direction, there is a chance the grizzly will go after you. If you run at these big red bears waving your arms and swinging your hat in an attempt to scare them off, eight times out of ten your bluff is not going to work. And then of course there is the odd chance that for some strange reason the grizzly's mind will go off the beam, he'll let out a rumbling roar that shakes the surrounding forests, and charge without any provocation.

If a hunter is hidden, a well-placed heart shot will often send an old grizzly on a wild roaring rampage before he falls dead, but shoot that same bear in the same spot with the same lead while he is looking at you, and he will travel a terrifying distance in your direction.

When Lester Dorsey of Anahim Lake guided a famous shot whom he called Ace to the Itcha Mountain grizzly whose measurements vied with the world's record, both men could easily have been killed had Lester not known his way around the big animals.

Ace and Lester spotted the grizzly when they were hardly seventy-five yards from him. The men looked upon a strange and most unusual sight. The big grizzly was mauling and buffeting around the body of a black bear which he had just killed.

Ace raised his gun. Lester snapped at him.

"Don't shoot yet! Quick—duck behind that hummock there. Don't let that bear see you—and don't move after you've made your shot."

Lester crawled into position behind another hummock about fifty yards from Ace with his gun ready.

The sportsman just couldn't believe that a heart shot or two wouldn't stop that bear within seventy-five yards, but he obeyed his guide. When he was ready Ace signaled Lester, took careful aim, and pulled the trigger.

The mountainous grizzly hit the ground roaring, came immediately to his feet, and charged in the direction of the sound of the shot.

He passed between both the hidden men going hell for leather, made another fifty yards before meeting a four-inch jackpine tree which he smashed in two with a paw, then tore to bits before falling over dead. You can imagine what would have happened had he spotted either man before he hit the dust for keeps.

From all I can find out, grizzlies, unlike black bears, have cubs only every other year. They roam the swamps and bush in close-knit family bands. Quite often there are from four to six bears in a group: the old boar, the mother, one or two cubs and quite often one or two two-year-olds.

With their inferior types of weapons, Indians had considerable trouble with grizzlies in the early days. Just when and why the Carrier and Chilcotin Indians put taboos on killing the big animals is not recorded, nor is it known why widely separated bands of Indians held different beliefs and superstitions about the central British Columbia grizzlies. It is possible that the oversized giants of the Itcha and Tatuk mountains and the Dean River valley, with their ferocity, canniness and power, gave old-time tribes such a bad time of it when they were wounded that the Indians found it wiser to study the grizzly's habits and stay safely away from him. The outcome of the grizzly-shooting taboo was that the bears had a good chance to multiply.

It was back in 1911 when Joe Murray, blue-eyed, rock-jawed, five-foot-six frontiersman from the state of

Arkansas, first heard of the Tatuk Lake country and the great abundance of fur-bearing animals that flourished in its dark jungles and spooky swamps.

One of the first white men to pioneer the area where the village of Vanderhoof now sprawls, Joe was fascinated with the tales the Indians brought back from Tatuk Lake, an estimated fifty unknown miles to the south. The natives constantly referred to the savage red and brown bears of that district, and Joe suspected that the grizzlies had spooked them out of there, leaving the mink and muskrat, fish, beaver, otter and lynx to multiply on a large scale.

The lure of that unknown country and the rewards to an experienced trapper proved too much for Joe. In November of 1911, he took the lonely plunge and arrived at the blue waters of Tatuk Lake just before freeze-up. His catch of upland and water fur piled up during the winter.

It was a balmy day early in May when Joe and his mongrel dog, Nig, set out on foot to pull up traps. On different occasions Joe had noticed numerous claw-fronted grizzly tracks in and around a big muskeg but he had had no run-ins with the animals as yet and gave little heed to the fresh marks that crisscrossed the muskeg on this particular day. Only once did he stop to examine a grizzly mark. It had been made by a particularly large animal. Joe stepped in the heel end of the track. His number-eight logging boot looked very small inside of it—almost half the size.

The hair on the back of Nig's neck stood up like a porcupine as he sniffed into the faint breeze. Joe carried on with his trap lifting, throwing each one into a sack dropped over his shoulder.

When Joe Murray bent down to break loose one of the last of his traps on the edge of the muskeg, he heard the brushing, scraping noises of bodies padding through the bush, the muffled crunch of soft, heavy feet on springy ground, and at the same time the rank smell of grizzly fur filled his nostrils.

A nerve-tingling sensation ran down Joe's spine. Less than ten paces away from him—five of the dreaded red grizzlies were shuffling towards him. Three were full grown, their hair standing straight up along their backs.

Joe had barely enough time to disentangle himself from his sack of traps when the great bulk of an enormous male was upon him. Joe sidestepped the grizzly and at the same time smashed his gun barrel at the animal's head.

The bear was upon him. Joe was upended. Before he lit on his back he stuck his gun barrel into the grizzly's mouth and pulled the trigger.

Joe remembers the roars of the bear—the great hairy arms swinging around him—the horrid odor of the beast's breath in his face, the rank smell of freshly squirting blood in his nostrils—and he heard Nig, the mongrel dog, barking and barking.

Joe realized that this was not just a bad dream. His head had been in the grizzly's gigantic mouth and the one shot he had fired must have broken the animal's jaw or Joe would not have been alive. With superhuman effort he struggled to his feet, and with the exertion his mind began to clear.

Fifty feet away the great male grizzly was charging the dog. The other bears stood a short distance off to one side, two large females up on their hind legs.

Joe realized that one of his eyes was gone—and when he reached up to touch his head he drew his hand quickly away as he felt the gaping blood-filled crack in his skull and the splintered bones of his head.

With his one eye Joe looked around for his gun, but the gory blood-belching figure of the grizzly was reaching out for him again. Joe pressed in close to the hairy body in front of him trying to avoid the terrific swings of the animal's paws, any one blow of which would have cut him in two.

The trapper went down again. Darkness was closing in—and the dog's bark was growing faint in the distance.

Painfully Joe swung his head and saw a jackpine tree perhaps two paces away from him. He staggered towards it as the enraged bear came up fast on the other side.

Wide, razor-sharp, claw-studded paws crashed into the tree. But the bulwark was not enough to keep man and bear apart for long. Joe remembers how he regained consciousness, flat on his back on the blood-spattered ground. In the distance he could hear the yakking of the dog and then he saw his leg through the torn trousers, a gash that looked as if a dull axe had been driven into the bone. He tried to rise but there was no reaction of bone or muscle or nerve in his leg. It was as limp as a paper doily.

Joe doesn't know how long he lay there, but at last he heard a low whine and felt Nig's hot wet tongue on his face. He crawled stiffly to his feet and surveyed the scene of the battle.

His rifle was nowhere in sight. He floundered awkwardly about looking for it through his one eye, then realized that no time could be wasted in his battle for life.

His hope of survival lay in the possibility that he could struggle more than forty miles through the mountains and muskegs to the Stony Creek Indian village.

With Nig limping behind him, Joe slugged through for a half mile to his trap cabin. There, he glanced at himself in a little pocket mirror. Whether or not his left eye was still intact behind a clotted mass of blood that ran from the back of his head over the top of his skull and down over the eye, he did not know. He found two clean dry towels and wrapped, then tied them tightly over his head, leaving only the side of his face with the one good eye exposed.

He tourniqueted his badly mangled leg and wrapped another towel around it. Then Joe prepared for the long ordeal that lay ahead. He packed matches, a Hudson's Bay blanket, and carried a long-bladed hunting knife in his belt. The dog limped along at his master's heels. The dark forest night closed in about them.

Joe had cut out nine miles of passable trail in a northerly direction towards Stony Creek, intending to finish it out during the summer. He surprised himself when, some time during the night, he came to the end of the trail. There were still about thirty miles to go.

The frontiersman rolled up in his blanket and tried to rest. In the cold dawn of a new day Joe dragged himself northward towards Stony Creek.

Some time towards evening Joe smelled smoke, noticed cinders falling like snowflakes around him, and far up ahead saw a boiling cauldron of black smoke puffing into the sky. The possible chance that he could some way make it through to Stony Creek seemed to be taken from him, for now a forest fire blocked his way.

Joe changed his course. He limped slowly on in a north-easterly direction. He groped his way through a heavy ground smoke and came suddenly out of the green timber to a mass of smoldering windfall that reached as far as the eye could see. The forest fire had swept to the west of him, leaving in its wake a desolate pile of dead smoking down timber—a big stretch of impassable terrain that still blocks off that country even today.

Joe walked and crawled along the fallen logs into the rising smoke. In places he was twelve feet off the ground. If he had made one misstep, he would never have been able to struggle up out of the tangled mass of still-burning logs and embers below him.

As twilight settled over the land on May 22, in 1912, the blood-caked figure of Joe Murray swayed into Billy Mathison's cabin on Nulki Lake. Mathison, who had been a first-aid man for a mining outfit in the Yukon, went into action. Tommy Blair, another old-timer, and Mrs. Lamont, a neighbor, acted as his assistants. Tommy Blair told me that they went to work on Joe's eye first, and that Joe had a total of over fifty wounds on his body. Miraculously, the sight of Joe's eye was saved, but the muscles in the forehead and eye were severed, and the lid still covers the eye. A scar an inch deep runs from Joe's cheekbone up through his forehead to the top of his skull.

It was twenty years almost to the day of the great grizzly fight when another trapper, Mansell Griffin, killed the famous Joe Murray grizzly. He shot the behemoth only three miles from the scene of Joe's and Nig's battle. The bear was identified by his broken lower jaw. His reddish skin measured over twelve feet in length, just a few hairs from the world-record hide. It was exhibited in Vanderhoof for several weeks.

When I parted from Joe a short time ago, the last thing I said was, "Tatuk Lake must have been a tough country back in those days."

"Yes," replied Joe, "the old-time Indians were right. It was a hard country to live in, but a mighty easy one to die in."

Now with the thought of Joe Murray's grizzly fight coming freshly to mind, I was a bit shaky as I went about gathering wood in the dark shadows of the windfalls. I turned the horses loose in the holding corral, got the fire going full blast, packed up a pot of water from the creek for my coffee, and prepared the evening meal.

What I did that night at Camp 44 to insure my life and future health was very simple. I dragged in a big pile of old stumps, roots, and down timber, started a huge bonfire blazing up into the darkness and kept it going all night. I rolled my sleeping bag out on the ground near the fire and grabbed off several hours' sleep between my stoking-up operations.

I have never heard of grizzlies, moose, cougars or wolves venturing close enough to a big fire to work over a human being.

The only spooky event of the night took place a short time before daylight. I awoke with a start to the sound of a heavy body crashing through the brittle windfalls out in the dark beyond the light of the fire. I heard the horses snort and then their hoofs pounding the ground along the corral fence, and then there was silence. The noise might have been made by a moose, but the chances are that the grizzly was at that time heading back to the trail. The following day his big tracks continued on down the trail almost to the Batnuni Valley, then swung off into the first row of high side hills. At that season of the year I suspect he was en route to the bunch-grass range, where he would feed on the lush new green bunch grass and occasional worm-glutted rotten stumps.

Strange as it may seem, in all the years that I ran cattle in grizzly-dominated country, I have never lost a cow or a calf to grizzlies—and yet have seen any number of moose completely demolished by them.

CHAPTER VII

The Happy Hunting Ground

FOR SEVERAL YEARS it had been our custom to trail around five hundred head of cows and their calves twenty miles up Batnuni Creek, to the headwaters of Big Bend Creek, where I spent each summer riding herd.

I now threw up my summer camp there directly beneath a long series of open bunch-grass hills that rose a half mile to a high flat plateau. This bench and the side-hill series ran for miles in a northeast and southwest direction on the back trail of a long-vanished glacier route.

The benchland looked as if it were weighted down by the enormous growth of rich grasses. Milk- and fat-producing legumes, pea vine and vetch, grew in an interlocking tangle three and four feet high. The pea-vine and vetch tangle combined with wild beans, wheat grass, redtop and wild millet. Most of these other grasses seem to thrive wherever the legumes sweeten rich black, leaf-moldy soils. The whole matted mass of vegetation grew in such profusion that it was actually impossible in many spots to break through it on foot. Even a horse would tire if he had to trip and stumble through miles of this grassy tangle.

While I camped with the cows on upper Batnuni, the

yearlings and the two-year-old steers that would be ready
for market in the fall were moved down country from
the ranch to the other side of a log drift fence, where
they fanned out between the drift and McNutt place.
Here they could be located at various salt licks almost any
time a rider did his checking for porcupine quills in face
and nose, spoiled bags which needed milking out, lark-
spur poisoning, snagged hoofs and the many other range
afflictions that had to be remedied.

Between our up-valley and down-valley range drift
fences sprawled a chunk of bunch-grass and park-land
range, sprinkled with the sage family's little cousin,
wormwood, a great horse and cattle tonic in early
spring. This ideal spring range was eight or nine miles in
length and from half a mile to two miles wide.

To fence all this country took a bit of scheming. When
we first took over the Batnuni, I spread the word around
that I would hire all Indians who wished to work on fence
contract, for log fence and the hanging Russell fence.
Often entire families worked at the job, old men, women
and children. These groups worked long into the night
and slept late in the morning.

My specifications called for fence at least six feet high.
One day the entire Indian population of Nazko arrived at
Batnuni, some fifteen wagonloads of men, women, children and babes in arms. I assigned them to a big flat a
mile down-country from the ranch buildings, named
Poison Creek. When their tents and teepees were all up,
the flats became a sizable village.

My Indian foreman, John Jimmy John, took charge. I
paid $175 a mile for worm fence, a type of log fence, and

$100 a mile for Russell fence, with the Company fur-
nishing the wire.

There's nothing like a neat, well set-up camp to keep
up morale. I prided myself on my summer cow camp. I
rigged up a twelve-by-twelve tent on a log-frame base
three to four feet high. Running over the top of the tent
and extending another ten feet out in front of it, I stretched
a heavy-duty sixteen-ounce canvas fly. Out under this
open-air kitchen-dining room were a small board writing
table, an eating table and log stools. On top of the outdoor, rock-enclosed fireplace that was built just under
the fly roof, rested an iron-latticed grill. I kept a long
high pile of kindling and stove wood split and stacked
under one edge of the fly.

Inside the tent, at one corner, was a foot-deep pile of
hay which I had slashed down with a hunting knife.
This was my mattress. My sleeping bag covered it. Two
apple boxes made up end-tables for a coal-oil lantern,
books and pocket emptyings. It was a very comfortable
summer home.

Supplies, stock salt and tools were stacked in one end
of the tent, and I built a crude rack for drying out wet
clothes. Even in wet rainy weather the tent was dry, warm
and comfortable.

Not more than 150 yards from camp, I built a log raft
on the edge of a small rock-bottomed lake with Batnuni
Creek flowing in one end of it and out the other. This
lake and the creek at each end were loaded with rainbow
trout measuring from half a pound up to three pounds.
The lake bottom was lined with a red-colored slate-type

rock, and the trout were a brilliant reddish-gold color, almost identical to the lake bottom. Their meat was as red as sockeye salmon and firm and fat. Needless to say, I practically lived on fish all season.

Late in the summer, hundreds of thousands of land-locked salmon ranging in color from pale trout green to dark green to purple to brilliant lacquer red, filled the creek from bank to bank. The Indians called these beautiful little fish Kokanee.

I used to set small net traps in shallow spots on the creek during the salmon runs. I only kept the dark-colored fish, enough to last several meals, and always turned the rest loose again.

From the tent camp I watched herds of game move out of the surrounding grassy park-lands to the lake shore to fight flies and drink. As many as eight moose at a time would wade into the lake until only their heads remained above water. Often moose would duck their heads beneath the surface to feed on water grass and weeds that grew on the lake bottom.

It was a strange sight to see moose heads, shoulders and flanks come popping up out of the smooth glassy surface of the water. I have seen three families of black bears throwing out salmon with their front paws. These families were fishing within fifty yards of each other. There were five bears including three cubs in one family, and four bears each in the other two. Thirteen bears—romping, playing, swimming and fishing all in one big happy-go-lucky group.

Deer were ever present. They would arrive in the open park en route to the lake all through the long daylight hours, singly, in pairs, and often in herds of six to twenty-eight. There were the tiny little white-tailed jumping deer that would make about four meals for one man, magnificent, wide-eyed, lovable little creatures, not much larger than a big jack rabbit, miniature deer who could jump clear over a seven-foot-high windfall.

There were other larger deer, what breed I don't know, who visited cow camp lake, and then bands of big mule deer, some bucks carrying massive sets of horns. They would water at the lake shoulder to shoulder with their tiny diminutive cousins, the jumpers. I cannot bring myself to kill deer or bear at any time, and game became almost tame.

Once several family groups of great fat black and gray timber wolves padded into camp in the early-morning hours. I counted twenty-two in the combined packs, but I know I didn't see them all. I welcomed the invaders with a bombardment from my 30.06. I jumped a saddle horse, and escorted them out of our happy valley with wild yells and stray shots. I don't think I hit one of them, but at least they didn't return the rest of the summer to the quiet little retreat.

Late that same fall, some thirty or forty of what we call the great northern wolves swept through our down-valley Batnuni range, hamstringing and killing or crippling some thirty head of steers, heifers and fat young cows. I have no idea how many calves they killed, devoured or packed away. On that same foray they cut out a four-and-five-year-old pinky-gray Belgian team from a band of fifty range horses. This was a matched team of mares and their two sorrel colts

were sired by our imported registered Clydesdale stallion. From the shattered trees, torn-up ground, and the
great ugly patches of blood splashed across the top of
the high side hill where the battle had taken place, I
knew that the two full sisters had put up a terrific fight
for their colts—only twisted bones and hoofs remained
of the mares. Even their skins had been devoured.
Wolves who have once experienced the taste of horse
meat prefer it above all other flesh.

My cow camp and the surrounding countryside
never seemed to cause that kind of a listless homesicky
feeling that has gripped me often when I was alone for
long stretches at a time. This balmy grass-, game- and
fish-infested land comes close to what I hope will be my
happy hunting grounds in the next world.

I never built corrals or a holding pasture at the Happy
Hunting Grounds. Any extra time that came my way I
spent fishing or exploring new country, but the grassy
flats around the camp afforded excellent staking places
for a wrangle horse, and I strung up a two-strand-rope
corral to catch my horses in.

Every two weeks, when I rode down to Batnuni to
pick up provisions and stock salt, I would return to cow
camp with an unbroken horse to straighten out. The
unridden range horses were always broken to lead before
I got them to cow camp. We would throw a heavy cow-
hide-boxed pack on the wild-eyed bronc, and by the time
I reached camp the animal would be sore-shouldered
from crashing into trees with his wide pack, and quite
anxious to lead up behind my saddle horse, staying carefully in the middle of the trail.

I would stake the bronc out close to camp where he would crash around and tangle himself up in the rope, but gradually he would know what a rope was. The following morning with a much-subdued colt to work on, I would cinch my saddle down hard on his back, cheek him around in a circle as I eased into the saddle, and start him plunging up the steep half-mile-high side hill that rose into the sky immediately in back of camp.

The enormous amount of wind and stamina that the horse required to fight his way to the top of the incline took so much concentration and physical effort on his part, that all thought of bucking, rolling on top of you or flipping over backwards was quickly forgotten. At the end of the bronc's two weeks' summer school, I would ride him and lead the pack horses down to Batnuni Ranch for my supplies.

It was a nice easy method of breaking out and gentling a few of the many unbroken mares and geldings that ran out on the Batnuni range.

The Frontier Company was heavy on horses, but they gave us little trouble, for their range was usually in remote swamps, meadows and side hills seldom used by the cattle. The range horses never had to be fed hay, but rustled out all year round, foaled without help, and led their own lives the way they wished.

It was late in the summer. My riding job was over. My wagon was loaded with a mowing machine, rake and haying equipment I had bought from the Company. Along with Mike and Bud, I headed back over the mountains towards Rimrock and Gloria.

———

I just couldn't believe what I saw as Mike and Bud lugged the machinery-loaded wagon into Rimrock with Rhino and the Blue Cheyenne and Giant tied by their halter shanks to the rear of the wagon box. The whole aspect of the place had undergone such a face lifting that there was little resemblance to the junk-bound ramshackle layout we had encountered when we had taken over.

The ranchhouse had been straightened up, with new log stringers replacing the old rotten ones on which the house had rested. The back porch had been enlarged and turned into a bright new glass-enclosed kitchen and dining room. Green asphalt shingles covered the roof, and a shanty-roofed bunkhouse log addition had been built on to the kitchen and pantry.

On the far side of the ranchhouse, I could see one corner of a glassed-in sun porch-sitting room. Short green grass surrounded the buildings where horses had been allowed to graze to mow the lawns.

A short distance beyond the ranchhouse I saw the walls and roof of a large one-room log cabin under construction. Neat new improvements, including a sumptuous reading room-outhouse stood out in immaculate relief against the lush green of horse-clipped lawn and lacy diamond willow clumps.

Before I had time to jump down off the wagon seat the Bear came roaring around the house and jumped on my chest as I hit the ground, with such force that I was catapulted back into the rumps of Mike and Bud. Then Gloria came dancing out of the new back door of the house. Her long blond hair accentuated her dark copper-color tan. I greeted Aunt Kate and the Queen who appeared around a corner of the house.

For the next few weeks I helped Sam finish off the log cabin, and assisted him and Gloria as they tacked up heavy-duty wallboard paneling inside the main house. I also rounded out my ditching operation which had dropped the lake four feet, uncovering some two hundred acres of rich black lake-bottom soil. Already a fine stand of grass had sprouted.

CHAPTER VIII

A Woman Who Won't Take Orders

GLORIA HAD ONE BAD FAULT—a dangerous one in the back reaches of a rough unpredictable land where you are not allowed many mistakes. No matter what the emergency she never took orders from anyone. She relied only upon her own judgment and resources. I had quite often suspicioned this trait of Gloria's but when I found it out for sure it was almost too late. Once, on a trip from Rimrock to Vanderhoof, she and I were riding our saddle horses, leading three pack horses tied head to tail. This was a quick, exhilarating trip. We covered the thirty-five miles, on hard horses, in five hours. I was leading the pack horses, riding Rhino; Gloria was riding Stuyve. The horses knew they were coming in to pasture, and were up on their toes, dancing impatiently to get over to my mother's house for green grass and rest. On one of her visits to British Columbia she had bought an eight-room log house on three acres of land a stone's throw in back of Reid's Hotel.

Her Frontier House was a godsend to both man and horse on our trips to town, and as usual, the horses were champing on their bits to get to her clover and bluegrass lawns.

Gloria was riding beside me. She is shortsighted, and no judge of distance or timing.

We were riding a short cut and had reached the railroad tracks. I looked down the rails and saw an approaching train some two hundred yards away. I judged it to be traveling at around thirty miles an hour. I could see it was a long freight, probably sixty to seventy cars—a mile long.

There was no problem. Lots of time to ride safely across the tracks to the other side.

As our saddle horses took their first step onto the tracks, Gloria got panicky.

"That train's too close," she screamed at me. "We can't make it!"

"Don't get excited, kid," I snapped at her. "We've just about made it now, and there's still a hundred and fifty yards between us. Stay right alongside of me. Easy, girl."

Suddenly and without any warning, Gloria swung Stuyve around and jumped back to the opposite side. I was safely on the far side of the tracks with the pack horses almost as quickly as Gloria reached her side. I swung in my saddle.

Now there were only seconds to spare, the engine was coming up fast.

I yelled at her. "Turn that horse away from the train. Spur him away from it!"

That was all I had time to say. The train roared between us.

Now another of Gloria's weaknesses became evident. Although she was adept at managing me, she consistently allowed a horse to boss her around. She exercised little firmness with her mounts. They did exactly what they pleased—and when. Gloria always went along with the horse. In this case, it was almost fatal.

As car after car flashed by, I caught glimpses, between cars, of what was happening on the other side of the mile-long freight. Instead of following my last order to turn Stuyve away from the train and spur him in the opposite direction, she had let him have his way—almost. I saw him dancing up and down—crowhopping. Being hotheaded, hotblooded and panicky himself, he was trying desperately to jump between the fast-moving cars to reach the other horses.

But Gloria had just enough grip on her bridle reins.

For the whole span of that long, long line of freight cars, I expected to see Stuyve, carrying an empty saddle, come crashing in between the couplings, and to know that Gloria was somewhere between the wheels, and there was just nothing I could do about it.

Miraculously, when the caboose finally went clattering past, Gloria, whose face had turned a trout green, was still up there in the saddle. Stuyve had witnessed his first train. He reached our sides in three long jumps.

At first I was in such a state of relief that I couldn't speak. We walked our horses up the street a block before I snapped out of it. Then I let fly a series of blasts that not only scared Gloria but spooked the horses into a run.

One spring day Gloria and I took Aunt Kate out across the meadow to show her part of the ranch.

It was the end of May. The sub-irrigated slough grass, wild redtop, bluejoint and timothy formed a thick green carpet that reached up almost to the knees.

Aunt Kate, who had spent a good deal of time on her own farm, knew soils and grass. She was greatly impressed with the black lake-bottom soil and the luxurious stand of grasses.

At the lower end where we crossed the meadow, it was a good half mile to the timber. Looking up-country, we could see nearly three miles of meadow grass as it weaved in and out of the clumps of bushes to disappear in a growth of giant diamond willows.

My mother-in-law was almost overwhelmed by the expanse of grassy meadow. This side of a stand of heavy spruce forest were several long rows of brush, recently slashed and piled in six-foot-high, fifty-foot-long wind-rows. Two hundred yards on the meadow side of the brush piles, a strange-looking type of weather-grayed sagging corral rose up above a pool of water and mud. Aunt Kate wondered what it was. I explained that the Dahl family had built this corral to house live beaver. The last fifty yards to the brush piles had to be crossed very carefully. Water-filled holes, three and four feet deep, were checkerboarded across this stretch of rough meadow.

We zigzagged our way through this obstacle barrier to the brush pile. Aunt Kate and Gloria sat down on a broken tree stump to rest. I looked up over the top of the brush pile towards the spruce jungle about 150 yards beyond us.

What I saw made my hair stand on end. Hardly sixty yards beyond our brush pile, between us and the spruce timber, two lean, long-legged cow moose were trotting up and down, throwing their ugly beaklike heads jerkily into the air, sniffing into the breeze, trying to locate the foreign smell that their sensitive moose nostrils had picked up.

This was a bad setup. One of the sinister-looking cow moose had a calf hidden some place. I could tell that from her actions and her shape. She was a very large animal. Her hair stood straight up along the hump in her back and her neck. Her hindquarters and flanks, lean and narrow, accentuated her deep gaunt chest. The other cow was much smaller and in better shape, probably a dry three-year-old.

There was a big chance that the old cow would charge without the slightest hesitation if she spotted us, particularly if the calf was hidden some place close to us. These thoughts flashed through my mind as I peeked between an opening at the top of the brush pile. If I had been on my own, I wouldn't have worried, but here were two women with me, and I suspected that Gloria wouldn't follow my directions.

Like a flash, numerous moose experiences crossed my mind. The long-headed, long-nostriled animals have a keen sense of smell. Their ears are sharp, but they have one failing—the eyes of a moose are weak.

There was no noticeable wind. Quickly I stuck my finger in my mouth and held it up in the air. A faint bubble formed reluctantly on one side of my finger, then disintegrated. Once more I licked my finger and held it up. This time a barely perceptible bubble formed on the other side. There was practically no breeze. Just a shifting draft that moved about from one direction to the other.

From my past experience, I calculated that there were nine out of ten chances that the mother cow would get a little more human scent, then, satisfied that her calf was not hidden between her and the unseen enemy, she would trot over to the timber, lick her calf to its feet, and lead it off—away from the contaminated area of man-smell.

We were well hidden behind the long brush pile. If we kept absolutely quiet and didn't make any movements for a few minutes, Mrs. Moose would probably vanish in the spruce jungle.

But if by any chance she spotted us at this stage of the game, there was a big chance she would charge. I have been up several trees, and so have many of my friends, with an angry cow moose at our heels.

Early in June, immediately after a calf is born, its mother is often fighting mad—afraid of nothing— dangerous, far more lethal than a bull moose in rutting season. A moose strikes out at its enemies with both front feet. Their hoofs are razor sharp, and they can hit with the power of a pile driver.

All these thoughts raced through my mind in a matter of seconds. Gloria and her mother were arguing about what to do with this section of the meadow, for if we wanted to use it as hay land, something would have to be done with the big water-filled holes and the rough hummocks.

Suddenly Gloria noticed me staring at something on the other side of the brush pile.

"What are you looking at?" she snapped at me, sudden panic showing in her face.

She started to jump to her feet, but I caught her by the shoulder and shoved her back down onto the stump. She knocked my hand away and started to rise again.

"Quiet now," I whispered. "Don't move, either of you."

I held Gloria down.

"There's nothing to worry about. Just do what I tell you. There's a couple of cow moose, one has a calf, they're over there beyond this brush pile. If we all stay quiet and don't move around, they'll trot away."

"I've got to see," cried Gloria.

"All right, Gloria, but get to your feet real slow so that there's no chance of the cows seeing any movement between this willow brush. And don't talk so damn loud! Whisper."

Gloria paid no attention to my warning. She sprung to her feet, breaking several dry willow sticks in the process.

"My God," she gasped when she saw the moose.

I looked through the brush pile. Both cows had swung around and were standing in their tracks, staring hard in our direction. The jig was up.

The cracking sticks, Gloria's high voice and her sudden movement had given away our position. Quickly I looked along the pile of brush for a long stick with a heavy root on the end. Something I could use as a club.

Aunt Kate had risen to her feet and, unlike Gloria, was calmly surveying the scene.

Gloria was a fast runner. She used to win most of the girls' foot races at the schools she attended, but no one can outrun a moose.

Suddenly and without any warning, Gloria took off across the pock-marked, water-hole-studded meadow.

"Come, Mother," she was yelling as she cleared the first water hole.

"Quick, Mother, run, run, run for your life!"

"Come back here, you idiot," I yelled at her. "We've got the brush pile to back against."

But it was too late. Aunt Kate looked around her, then took off in the wake of her daughter. I saw Gloria flounder into a water hole to her waist, but she was going so fast that she seemed to gain speed as she plowed out on the other side.

In the brief second in which the evacuation of brush pile took place, I had been unable to locate a club. I got a snap look at the moose. The big cow had her eyes glued to Gloria's flying figure. She pawed the ground, made several loud grunts and came in our direction at a trot, swinging her head up and down.

I took another flash look for a weapon. I swung around from the brush pile in time to see Aunt Kate, her dress floating around her shoulders, trying to crawl out of the first water hole she had encountered. She was in water almost to her shoulders—and having a bad time of it.

The big cow was only a few yards away from the brush pile now and coming fast, and then I heard a growl, low and menacing, rising up from a lone willow at one end of the barricade. It was the old Bear. He had been lying down under the willow, out of sight, no doubt waiting for my order. I had trained him never to take after moose, deer or bear, or cattle, unless I yelled, "Take 'em."

This time, however, the old boy took the law into his own hands. The cow moose was approaching us at too fast a clip to suit the dog's good judgment. Before I had a chance to yell, the Bear came out of his retreat with a roar of anger. In three jumps he circled the oncoming cow, got one bite at her heels, and the group of them—the young dry cow, the angry mother cow, and the Bear—disappeared in the timber.

I rushed to Aunt Kate's aid, pulled her out of the water hole and escorted her, cold and dripping, to the beaver pen, where Gloria sat on the top rail. I asked my mother-in-law to forgive me if I gave her daughter hell for not listening to my advice, and she told me to go right ahead.

The old Bear joined us with an amused expression on his face, his tail wagging back and forth over his head. The Bear took the lead, the moose incident already forgotten. We followed him safely back to the ranchhouse and the living room heater, without further adventure.

I remember another time that Gloria followed her own instinct rather than follow my advice.

One fall a couple of years later one of her brothers, Jack McIntosh, was up for a goose shoot. Jack, like his mother, sister and brother Fraser, was interested in soil, grass, forage crops and all the other ramifications of agriculture.

Gloria and I took him for a long walk up through the meadow, pointing out as we went along the improvements we had made, and describing in detail our myriad plans for further development and expansion.

We had reached a point some two and a half miles up-meadow from the ranch buildings, where a strip of sour soil had nursed a six-acre patch of buck brush to a height of five or more feet. Buck brush has an affinity for certain types of sour un-nitrogenous soils. The meadow here was three-quarters of a mile wide, bare of trees. We had stopped at the edge of the buck-brush patch for a discussion of some sort, when the grunting chant of a bull moose on the prod suddenly rose up out of the under-growth not more than fifty yards away.

This moose was really mad. I could tell by the tone of his voice and by the crash of bushes which he was uproot-ing and slashing into with his horns.

"Oh my God!" exclaimed Gloria. "Oh my God!"

"Down, everybody," I commanded. "Down to your knees behind this bush. He hasn't seen us yet, and he won't root us out with his smeller. We'll crawl back a few yards in case he comes looking for us out on the meadow."

Jack and I were down almost instantly, crawling into the bush. The moose was coming closer, making a ter-rifying noise. I wasn't too happy about the situation, particularly with Gloria along.

But my general reactions weren't quite fast enough. Hardly had Jack and I hit the ground before Gloria, with her dress streaking into the air behind her, shot out onto the meadow.

"Quick, Jack," she screamed. "We can't stay there, don't listen to Rich."

"For crying out loud," exploded Jack, "what the hell are we going to do now?"

He didn't wait for my answer. Jack was out on the open meadow himself, sprinting after his sister.

"Of all the crazy little fools I ever saw," I began to rage. "There they go, three-quarters of a mile to go to the crik—out in plain view of that rogue moose, and with a head start of not more than fifty yards."

All sorts of ideas flashed across my mind. But there was only one answer. My wife was out there, and in a few seconds so would be the moose, tramping her to death.

I jumped to my feet and lined out across the meadow. I could hear the moose noise stop suddenly, then a loud hissing sound. He had spotted our moving figures. He was in the middle of a crazy period in rutting, would attack anything on foot, save one animal, his mortal enemy, the wolf.

Then I could hear the brush cracking behind me. The moose was picking up a charge.

Then suddenly it dawned on me that the Bear had started out on this expedition with us. We had been so busy talking that I had forgotten all about him, but I knew he wouldn't desert and go home. He was probably lying down some place in that bush. For just a brief instant I skidded to a stop and started yelling.

"Take him out, Bear, take him out, Bear."

Forty yards away the moose was breaking clear of the buck brush. I didn't look back again. I heard a great turmoil behind me, the cranky roar and yak-yak-yak of the Bear, and startled grunts and bellowings of the surprised moose.

When I was a senior in high school, I had run the hundred-yard dash in 10.8 seconds flat in my football uniform and shoes. I did no better in my track shoes and shorts. It wasn't good enough time to get me more than third or fourth place in that event, but now I was to turn in a run that, if it had been timed, would have placed me among the immortal quarter-milers of all times.

Ahead of me, Jack was gaining on Gloria, who had had a fifty-yard start on him. Jack had at least a fifty-yard lead on me. I really went into action. As I quickly ate up the distance between Jack and me, I saw him go by Gloria as if she were standing still.

I thought to myself, I never knew Jack could run!

Later on I found out he couldn't, but on this occasion he was breaking all existing Vancouver and Pacific Coast records.

The dog and moose noise was growing faint in the distance as I raced past Gloria, caught up to Jack, went by him so quickly he thought it was the moose.

Then we could hear Gloria's voice far in our wake.

"Women and children first, boys," she was calling. "Women and children first."

CHAPTER IX

Gloria's Beef Drive

GLORIA'S FIRST BEEF DRIVE took place in the fall of 1944, when she, Harold Dwinnell, George Alec, the Trout Lake Indian, and I drove the Company beef from Batnuni to Vanderhoof.

Driving cattle in the rough and broken, heavily timbered country of British Columbia offers problems that one rarely runs into in the open or partially open country of the States and the prairie provinces of Canada.

While the herd moves towards its destination it is bad business to allow sidewinders to wander along in the brush and timber bordering the trails. It is even more disastrous to trail them all bunched up, causing them to spread and scatter out in a wide front. The cattle must be carefully maneuvered to string out singly or two abreast, never more than three abreast.

When you see a long thin line of cattle, one behind the other, walking along at their natural pace of one and a half to two miles an hour you will know that the cowhands handling those critters know their business, and that the herd will reach night camp without too much loss in weight. Camps are spaced from seven to ten miles apart.

Cattle will cover this distance in seven or eight hours including an hour's feed and rest period at a halfway point on a meadow or grassy swamp. In the evening the cattle will rest and graze for perhaps three to four hours.

At daylight they are again allowed to graze for two or three hours unless the weather is too hot; then it pays to hit the trail in the cool early-morning hours. In this easy-going manner, beef can be landed at railhead with little loss of weight even after a twenty-one- or twenty-two-day drive, the time it takes Pan to move his beef to the railroad from the Home Ranch.

There is only one system that works when an outfit is driving cattle down the long British Columbia wilderness trail. One man, usually the boss, breaks in from six to ten presumably intelligent and well-adjusted steers or old cows as the leaders on the first day of the drive.

When the leaders move ahead down the trail in front of the lead driver, the cattle behind will follow instinctively. On a small 160-head drive such as we started out with there should have been two center drivers, each behind fifty or sixty head, and a drag man to bring up the rear and watch the bush on both sides of the trail with a sharp practiced eye for sidewinders, stragglers, bunch-quitters or loners trying to sneak back through the bush.

As we left the ranch, I took the lead and began stringing, pushing and dropping back, then cutting more cattle to the front, all the while feeling out various individuals for my final choice of eight leaders.

For maybe an hour we adjusted ourselves and the beef herd to our positions on the drive. George Alec took center rider position and Harold maneuvered the drag, the toughest and most responsible position on a bush drive.

Gloria came behind leading three pack horses carrying our kitchen, bedrolls, tents, traps, axes and other needed equipment.

We had no trouble moving the beef the first three days, but on the afternoon of the fourth day out the trail herd balked at the sudden smell of a pack of black wolves who slithered across a swamp a short distance ahead of my leaders. Suddenly all hell broke loose. Cattle stampeded off in every direction. Most of them plunged into a swamp bog that bordered a narrow mud-banked creek. Ahead of us the trail zigzagged several hundred yards up a steep incline surrounded on both sides by high piles of down timber.

Several years before, a forest fire had swept through this part of the country killing all trees that lay in its path. Now most of the timber had fallen. Streaking through this blackened mass of fire-killed jackpines, the trail looked like a long narrow high-sided chute. I figured if I could get a bunch of steers into this chute I'd have them beat; they couldn't possibly get around my saddle horse here.

We splashed and plowed and jumped our mounts in, out and around the swamp at the bottom of the hill until through sheer horsepower and madness, we slugged nine big two-year-old steers into the narrow chute at the base of the steep hill. Then Harold and George Alec swung about and went after the other cattle. Over my shoulder I could see the backs and shoulders of two old cows and a steer struggling and plunging about in the grass-covered muck where they had bogged down.

I yelled at Gloria to tie the pack horses to a tree and ride up fast to give me a hand with the small bunch of green leaders I was holding in the chute in front of me.

Gloria worked fast. It didn't take her long to gallop Stuyve up alongside of me. The lead steers took one look at Gloria's brightly colored windbreaker and slacks and probably caught the scent of a female rider, heard her high woman's voice, and bang, they whirled around in their tracks and raced madly up the hill.

"Good girl," I barked hoarsely at Gloria. I had yelled myself down to a hissing whisper at this point.

"Stay right behind them now, girl, don't let them get too far ahead of you, but don't crowd them—and for God's sake, don't let them turn back on you and beat you out. I'll catch up to you pronto. We've got critters bogged down and steers scattered from hell to breakfast. Get going now."

"I'll do my best," Gloria called over her shoulder. "But what about those wolves?"

"Forget 'em," I yelled.

Stuyve took up the chute and over the hill in back of the leaders at a run. The last I saw of them, Gloria was leaning over her saddle, her hair and jacket flying out behind her. I swung Cheyenne around and went after the bogged cows.

Time slipped by. Harold, George, the old Bear and I were possibly an hour pulling cows out of the mud and throwing the other brush crackers back into the roundup. Finally with the Bear on one side of the assembled cattle and the three of us riding back and forth on the other flank, we managed to shove them into the chute on the tracks of the lead steers.

When we finally slammed the reluctant cattle over the top of the long hill they straightened out. My regular leaders, used now to being up in front where they were not crowded by other steers, worked towards their lead positions and when all were in their proper places I told George Alec I would leave the leaders with him, lope on down the trail and catch up to Gloria, our relief lead driver.

Cheyenne cracked into his long ground-gaining lope and the windfalls and the timber flashed behind us. I breathed in a sigh of relief. That had been a bad mix-up back there in the swamp. We could have gotten ourselves and the cattle into a lot of trouble, but luck was in our favor and we were away with no harm done and plenty of daylight left to make Bear Creek Meadow, our night camp.

The way I had it figured, Gloria and her nine head of spooked leaders had an hour's start on us. I was sure that following their fast dash up the hill, they would either settle down to their usual trail plod, probably average two miles an hour if Gloria didn't push them, or else they would balk some place along the trail, beat Gloria out and meet me as they dangled along on their back tracks towards home and the rest of the cattle.

I hoped that they wouldn't suddenly pretend a spook and head pell-mell into the bush with Gloria and Stuyve in hot pursuit, to wind up eventually in some unknown desolate spot in the wilderness tangle that sprawled out for miles in every direction.

I tried not to think about what Gloria's reactions would be if she wound up with a bunch of steers, darkness creeping down, wolves howling in the distance, and with the knowledge that she was lost for sure.

I was afraid that in her panic she would probably do the wrong thing, fail to let Stuyve have his head to lead her safely back to the trail and the other horses.

Cheyenne wanted to dangle. I gave him his head. The miles fell rapidly behind us.

Five miles beyond the beef drive I slowed Cheyenne down to a walk as I studied tracks. We were approaching the turnoff into Bear Creek Meadow, our camp grounds for this night. Tracks—those of the big steers and Stuyve's shod hoofs—carried on down the trail. From the spacing between tracks I realized that the bunch of them were still on the run.

I cursed loudly and let Cheyenne ease into a long ground-gaining lope. Bear Creek holding grounds dropped behind us. The next night's camp, 44, lay some nine miles ahead.

I didn't know how far Gloria and the steers would run before the group of them all played out. I had never been up against anything like this before.

"This is what I should have expected from a woman," I yelled at Cheyenne. "You just never know what the hell they're going to do next. If it's only remotely possible to find a way to ball things up, that's what's going to happen if you leave it to a woman."

44 Camp was coming up. Darkness wasn't far off. Cheyenne skidded around a bend in the trail, and there, not fifty yards beyond me, were Gloria and Stuyve and the steers trotting jerkily down the trail.

"You headin' for Vanderhoof?" I barked at Gloria. "You can't make it in one day, you know."

I turned Cheyenne into the bush and loped him around Gloria and her steers.

"About-face, you bunch of knotheads," I yelled.

I cut off the steers and they stopped in their tracks, their tongues hanging out, a purplish color, almost touching the ground in front of them.

"I didn't know how to stop them or turn them around," Gloria called to me. "They just kept trotting and running on down the trail."

She was breathing hard and looked frightened. Her face was white and her eyes tired looking.

"But at least I didn't lose one single animal. I've got them all here in one bunch. Every time they slowed down, one of the steers would turn around and look at me and then they'd all seem to panic and run down the trail again."

"You were crowding 'em too close," I told her, "and you let Stuyve do exactly as he pleased, keep stepping on their heels." I was still angry. "You've taken about a hundred pounds off each steer and caused them to drop down at least one grade."

"I did the very best I could," Gloria apologized, "and I did what I thought best under the circumstances."

Actually she had done the right thing by holding them together, a superb job for anyone not used to handling cattle.

"O.K., girl," I said. "Let's get traveling. We'll move them along slow and easy so they won't wind up too stiff or leg-weary. They're tender-footed already."

I cut Gloria in with the lead steers and drove the works of them back down the trail towards Bear Creek.

Five days later we eased the beef into the Vanderhoof stockyards. Gloria's first beef drive was ended. Harold complimented her on her big improvement in trailing cows and leading pack horses, and George Alec thanked her for the good meals she had produced along the trail.

CHAPTER X

Panhandle Phillips Pays a Visit

ONE DAY IN THE SPRING OF 1945, Gloria and I had just wearily bedded down at five A.M. in my mother's house after an all-night get-together with some of our Vanderhoof friends, when we heard the Bear's loud roar issue from the porch below. There was a moment's silence, then a wild, ear-splitting, nerve-shattering cowboy screech split the air. There followed another eerie pantherlike scream, the back door slammed open, heavy footsteps pounded up the stairs.

I said, "What the hell!" and there—staring down at us with a mischievous grin on his face—was flashing-eyed, hawk-faced, darkly tanned Panhandle Phillips.

"Up and out, you two bed-lovers," drawled the old Wild Horse.

For a moment I was completely stunned. Why had Pan Phillips slugged nearly two hundred miles of rough trail, crossed two mountain ranges, swum a river to get to Vanderhoof? Quesnel was Pan's supply town, and now the haying season was staring him in the face.

"Oh, it must be Pan!" exclaimed Gloria, rising to a sitting position in bed and pulling a dressing gown around her shoulders. "I can't believe it's really you!"

I rolled out of bed, and gave my old partner a resounding slap on the back of his heavy moosehide coat. The noise sounded like a rifle shot. Pan didn't seem to notice this warm greeting of mine.

"Shake hands with Aunt Gloria, Pan."

His impish grin, splitting his face from ear to ear, accentuated his long features and his high-bridged, eagle-like nose.

"Well, well, well," he said, reaching across the rumpled bedcovers to grasp Gloria's hand in his big black banana-sized fingers and broad rope-calloused palm.

"This sure explains why Rich here broke down after thirty-six years of toughin' it out alone, and done married the prettiest little blond girl in British Columbia."

Gloria actually blushed under Pan's openhearted compliment.

"This is just wonderful, Pan, to meet you at last. Every other sentence Rich utters is about his old partner, Wild Horse Panhandle. I'll tidy myself up a bit and cook you men up some ham and eggs. You must be starved, Pan."

"Not too hungry," apologized Pan, edging towards the bedroom door, "but I sure could go for a fast smash out of that liquor store you folks are running downstairs."

"Oh my, what a frightful mess we must have left the house in," sighed Gloria. "This is our first trip to town for three months and a lot of our pals came last night to celebrate. I'll be right down and clean up the wreckage."

Pan rested his hand on my shoulder as we walked down the stairway. I could see and feel that he heartily approved of my choice of a wife and this meant a lot to me.

"Boy, oh boy," he said. "You sure ain't fallin' down on your woman-savvy, son."

Pan grinned happily as his hand came in contact with a half-empty bottle of Scotch. His extrovert personality, brimming over with health, strength and big things in the making, seemed to charge the atmosphere around him and spread through the log house. He grabbed up two empty used glasses, splashed in generous portions of Scotch, handed me one and gravely raised his glass high in the air, peering through the liquid into the sunlight that streamed through the kitchen window.

"Down, friend," he said. "Down, down, down, friend. To old times."

Pan's glass-filled hand moved swiftly to his mouth and the liquid vanished. I looked at mine, gagged, then filled the drink with water from the tap. With a super-human effort I belted half of it down.

Pan refilled his glass with Scotch.

"You're slow, friend," he said. "Not leadin' the right kind of life. Here's to new times and to the new and beautiful bride."

Pan's hand moved almost as swiftly as he could pull his six-shooter from its holster. The glass of Scotch was emptied in one long gulp. I managed to get the rest of my drink down between gags and sputters. I set my glass down among the array of bottles, empty glasses and ash trays.

"You old raccoon," I bellowed at Pan. "What brings you across the range to this peaceful, restful little back-eddy town—and right at the start of haying?"

Pan took two long steps to the kitchen stove, lifted off the lid, grabbed up some kindling, peeled off some slivers with his pocketknife, struck a match to the tinder, replaced the lid and turned to welcome Gloria as she entered the room, all freshened up and raring to go.

"I'll tell you all about it, friend," Pan drawled to me over his shoulder. "We've got lots of time to powwow."

My vitality picked up somewhat, following ham and five eggs, a quarter of a loaf of bread and half a quart of milk.

Pan apologized in advance for his small appetite— particularly when he wanted to show Gloria how much he enjoyed her excellent cooking. He then proceeded to down ten fried eggs, a frying pan full of ham grease poured over nearly a pound of fried ham, and half a loaf of bread, and half a quart of milk.

Gloria was delighted, but also stunned, by Pan's enormous breakfast feat, but I knew what to expect.

Pan had been riding steadily now for four days and far into the night. He had covered two hundred miles, changing from one to the other of the two horses he brought with him. Out in the fenced-in back yard, I was somewhat surprised to see what good condition the two big geldings were in after their long grueling push from the Home Ranch. But Pan had a way of walking, trotting, occasionally loping his mounts over long distances without causing them to become too leg-weary or played out.

One of his tricks, I had found out years before, was a system he followed of alternating from four hours' steady riding, to three hours' feed and rest periods. He carried out this type of schedule day and night, and covered phenomenal distances with little harm done to the horses he rode.

Pan and I had a prodigious amount of Company business and future plans to go over together. The old Wild

Horse (a name he fell heir to in Wyoming where he spent most of his time chasing wild horses) was brimming over with smart ideas, short cuts, time-saving plans, the quickest and surest method of accomplishing this objective and that.

He was, and is, a mighty slick customer, with a razor-sharp brain and a photographic mind. No small detail ever seems to escape his dynamic conceptions. And, strangely, Pan was one of the few men I knew who would follow up any deal he had figured out, and carry it to its eventual termination.

I showed Pan several letters I had received from our Company lawyer, Arthur D. Crease, of Victoria. Mr. Crease had confirmed, in his correspondence with me, that my resignation had been duly accepted by our New York powers-that-be, and that Pan's resignation, to take place a year later, was also acknowledged and accepted.

But Mr. Crease had pointed out that, from the figures he had on hand, it would not pay to ship all the Company cattle from the Home Ranch unit.

This fall and the following year, after the high income taxes on the main bulk of the herd had been paid, the proceeds of the final breeding stock would automatically go to the government for taxes. Mr. Crease suggested that I start making plans to cut out at least two hundred head of cows and calves, feed them at Rimrock for two years before shipping them, and receive as compensation their calf crops for those two seasons.

Pan thought this a top idea and suggested that Gloria and I get the necessary hay in the stack that summer, and then fly back to the Home Ranch with Russ Baker in his Junkers. We could cut out the cows and calves that suited me, and later on, ride back in with a trail outfit to drive the critters to Rimrock Ranch.

We agreed on this plan and made a tentative date to meet at the Home Ranch the following year.

Pat Patterson joined Gloria, Pan, the old Bear and me for dinner at the house. Pan and Pat put on a real show. This pair of tongue-in-cheek, self-professed Irishmen from the United States and Canada could send you rolling on the floor in such spasms of laughter that your chest and stomach ached for days afterwards. The three of us escorted Gloria to the dance at a country schoolhouse that night.

The next evening Gloria and I waved au revoir to Panhandle Phillips as he mounted his big bay saddle horse and, leading the unpacked relay horse behind him, disappeared behind the Reid Hotel on the first lap of his two-hundred-mile journey home. In his saddle pockets were two pounds of bacon, a loaf of bread and a half pound of coffee, the sum total of his provisions for the many strenuous trail days that lay before him.

"Pan's just perverse, and he's so damn tough, he just likes to test himself out," I explained to Gloria, who couldn't grasp Pan's refusal to take any more grub with him. "When he arrived here yesterday morning, he'd been on the trail all night. Nothing to eat for twenty-four hours. Altogether he'd been riding for four days and four nights on a half pound of coffee, one loaf of home-made bread and a pocketful of moose jerky."

"Now I understand why Pan ate such prodigious meals during the short time he was here," reflected Gloria. "He was replenishing an empty larder on his ride out to Vanderhoof, and stoking up a surplus for his return."

CHAPTER XI

A Bride for Pan

IN THE FALL OF 1944 I had made arrangements with the Frontier Cattle Company to buy sixty head of heifers and a bull from them. This would be our nucleus breeding herd. We borrowed $3,000 from the bank to pay for the cattle, then I saddled up and, accompanied by sixteen-year-old Walter Erhorn, struck out for Batnuni to drive the heifers, bull and my string of sixteen horses out to Rimrock.

Trailing out the mixed bunch of cattle and horses in one group was a tricky and ticklish job. Most of the two- and three-year-old colts were unbroken, wild and hard to hold together on the trail. I don't believe we would have landed the stock at Rimrock without the help of the old Bear, who turned in a terrific performance keeping the snuffy heifers out of the bush and off the back trail, while Walter and I were continually heading off the fast-running loose horses in the lead of the drive.

It took us thirteen days to move this outfit the esti-mated hundred miles from Batnuni to Rimrock, using a short cut side trail that branched southwest from the Vanderhoof road at Elijah Hargreaves' homestead. On the height of land at four thousand feet elevation, near the confluence of the Tatuk Mountain creeks and the Nulki brooks, the weather clamped down on us. Low-lying gray-black clouds settled down around our unhappy trail drive and proceeded to belch out nearly a foot of soft, extremely wet snow. We were unable to warm up or dry out for a week.

When we finally came out of the mountains beyond Elijah Hargreaves' farm, on the shortcut trail to Rimrock, both the horses and the cattle stampeded when one of the leaders ran into the first barbwire fence any of the stock had ever seen.

A group of well-meaning country ladies rushed out of their farm homes to give us a helping hand. They waved aprons, towels and brooms in the direction of our range heifers and wild horses. That was all these spooky animals needed. Monumental action ensued. The frightened stock crashed through, uprooted and tore down a mile of barbwire fence, miraculously escaping without any serious injuries.

It was at the start of this fiasco that I permanently alienated those charming women who had come to our aid by a roaring bellow of profanity which issued forth as I raced madly through their fences and yards, destroying flower and vegetable gardens.

It was a tired, wet, cold bunch of horses, cows and men that shuffled wearily down into Rimrock Ranch, but we were at last in business. We had landed the stock.

During Walter's and my absence, Herman Weinhardt and Walter Erhorn's brother Neil had put up more than 150 tons of hay for us on the Rimrock meadows. This would be more than enough to winter our newly acquired herd and our string of horses, most of which would paw out their own feed around the Rimrock Lake. I traded a couple of saddle horses to Neil and Herman for their haying labor, paid Sam Goodland off for his superb summer construction jobs around the ranch, and Gloria, Walter Erhorn and I settled down to the long winter that stretched ahead of us.

Walter and I quickly knocked over two young, fat and tasty moose for our winter's meat and hung the eight front and hind quarters up in our newly built meat house. Gloria was ecstatic about the addition of our new little herd of top heifers and she pranced and danced about the neat and attractive ranch buildings which she had worked on for the past six months. She acted like a child with a batch of newly acquired toys. She traded Margaret Weinhardt (Herman's wife), our next-door neighbor, who lived three miles away, some furniture for six hundred pounds of baking potatoes, a hundred pounds of carrots, twenty cabbages and a lean two-hundred-pound pig which we put into a wooden barrel with a ham-smelling mixture called Habacure.

Now all we needed to live like kings for the winter was flour, yeast, baking soda, beans, rice, coffee and tobacco. But we also required the money to buy these delicacies. Gloria and I went over our inadequate ranch-style books and were quite shaken to find our puny bank account had somehow swapped ends on us and we were now on the red side of the banker's ledger and beyond the point of borrowing more money on what assets we had.

My mother was in New York and Gloria's mother, Aunt Kate, had returned to her home in Vancouver, and they were the last people on earth that we wanted to cry to for help as we had constantly bragged to them about our good business acumen and independence, and had condemned the new generation who wouldn't pioneer and expected their families to supply them with luxuries as well as necessities.

Gloria and I decided to ride to town and somehow, some way, straighten out our finances and figure a way to buy our supplies for the winter. We ran into a streak of luck. At the post office, mixed in with a monumental pile of the usual bills and bad news, was a letter from Skook Davidson from Lower Post on the Yukon border with a check for $480 enclosed and a letter explaining that he was relying on us to winter one of his pack strings, sixteen head of horses which would arrive shortly in the Vanderhoof area. At the time Skook was the British Columbia government guide and packer in the northern wilderness where surveys for timber, minerals, oil and future roads were being run.

Four hundred and eighty dollars in those days was a small fortune and would go a long way on a ranch. Our winter food problems were solved. The future looked bright. Gloria and I loped back to Rimrock in high spirits, secure in the knowledge that we were able to pay Walter his $30 a month wages, winter our stock and Skook's horses, and concentrate on piling up our year's wood supply and the five thousand fence rails and four hundred logs that we needed to make a workable cattle operation.

That was a fine winter. Only once did the mercury register fifty below zero. Then it kindly tapered off to thirty below and soon gave us the break of a thawing period. There were no losses among our horses or cattle, dogs or the three humans assembled at Rimrock Ranch.

Early in the summer of 1945, a few months after the famous meeting in Vanderhoof, I received a letter from Pan and with Gloria's help I deciphered his scrawl. The message on a crumpled piece of white wrapping paper read like this:

Anahim Lake

To Blackwater Playboy—
Hello Friend Rich—I am at Dorseys lining up load of freight. Expecting you up to cut out those cows for lease to Rimrock. How did you winter boy. My cattle wintered good. Bought me a thoroughbred stallion to cross on Wangleather's fillies. He is sure a dandy.

Pan

P.S. I forgot to tell you I got married. Her name is Betty and she's good looking girl—likes the bush. Betty says tell Rich to bring Gloria to Home Ranch on plane with Russ Baker—and I say bring 2 bottles O.P. rum too. Good riding. *Your Pardner.*

When I received Pan's letter we suddenly realized it was time to get Russ Baker and his old Junkers to fly in to the Home Ranch. Time was marching on and the cows for Rimrock should be cut out of the Home Ranch herd. Gloria and I left Walter Erhorn at the ranch and rode into town on Stuyve and Rhino to prepare for the Home Ranch trip.

CHAPTER XII

Sky Party Over Batnuni

MAYNARD KERR AND RUSS BAKER had flown together a great deal during the past summer in search of cinnabar outcroppings. It dawned on Maynard that it would be a sound idea to establish a flying agency for the pilot and his Junkers. Now the merchant was advertising bush flying and inaugurating a flying service from Fort St. James to Prince George and other points north, in addition to his other activities. Maynard was the man to contact for a chartered-plane trip into the remote Home Ranch. I rode up the street to the Kerr grocery store.

There were no hitching rails on the Vanderhoof main street. A group of small kids hung around the street corners picking up an odd dime for holding saddle and pack horses for ranchers and packers who arrived in town to do their shopping.

I jumped off Rhino in front of the store and handed a young boy my bridle reins. As I pushed through the door I noticed one of the window displays. It was a real eyecatcher. A specially constructed toilet complete with seat, and hooked into a heavy-duty iron septic tank of the chemical variety.

Maynard's young store manager met me at the door

and walked with me back to the office. Maynard was sparkling with smiles, health and good humor. He poured me a fast drink of Scotch and soda and, while I was sipping it, told me with a great burst of enthusiasm about one of his latest business adventures.

"I've just landed the agency for backwoods cabin toilets, Rich. It's a big deal. For every log cabin, an indoor toilet. That's the Kerr motto.

"There are only fourteen indoor toilets in Vanderhoof. All the rest of the houses have outdoor plumbing. Why, I'm telling you, Rich, this is a revolutionary advancement for North Country living. An inducement to every family who plan to move up here. I'm going to advertise this toilet setup in every paper north of Kamloops. Hundreds—no, thousands—of cabins and shacks scattered across the Northland should have an indoor toilet. The cost is nothing, practically nothing."

"How much are these wonders, Maynard?" I asked. "Around here not many cabin owners have enough cash to buy a water bucket."

"One hundred and ninety-nine fifty." Maynard beamed. "Less than two hundred dollars. Think of it—and a family has comfort for life! A feeling of social advancement, after their primitive lives."

Maynard ushered me down a long aisle flanked by stands weighted down with groceries, past a huge deep freeze display case, and up to the front window where the new Maynard Kerr toilet, wonder of the North, competed with selected delicacies from the South.

"What I'm here for, Maynard, is not to buy a toilet but to arrange through your airplane agency a chartered-plane trip to the Home Ranch. Tomorrow or the next day, if possible, I've got to get in contact with Pan, and fast."

Maynard rightabout-faced, waved his hand at me.

"Look over that disposal system," he called over his shoulder. "I'll line Russ up immediately."

The front door opened. Pat Patterson strutted through the door. He held it open for a moment to let the important-looking Bear enter. I had left him outside on purpose. Because of Maynard's good-natured hospitality the Bear had been taking undue advantage of him.

The big blacksmith was clad in what he always termed his formal clothes. A grease-smeared pair of coveralls with many pockets, tool holders, snaps and rings, bulging with wrenches, claw hammers, ball-pin hammer, cold chisel, screwdriver, assorted nuts and bolts and scrap iron of all sizes and weights.

On his jet-black hair the fifty-year-old ironman wore his usual black visorless skullcap. His deep heavily muscled chest and corded biceps bulged beneath his party clothes. Patterson walked towards me, no expression on his face, his thumbs hooked under his wide leather suspender straps.

I left my position near the toilet display and stepped towards the blacksmith.

"Why you old coyote, how the hell are you?" I yelled with delight. "Was just going to head for the blacksmith shop."

Pat looked very serious. He strode past me, his eyes glued to the window, stopped, and swung his head from side to side.

"Civilization creeping into the North Country," Pat

sighed. "Maynard will ruin this land with his modern ideas."

Maynard came bustling towards us, his face wreathed in smiles.

"Wonderful news, Rich. Russ Baker is gassing up the Junkers and will pick you up in two hours. He's got nothing lined up for today."

Pat broke in. He was still concentrating on the Kerr toilet.

"Maynard, you're taking chances here in your grocery department. Some damn fool's gonna think you've set this water closet up as a convenience for your customers, and use it."

"I'll put up a sign—Out of Order," Maynard put in hurriedly.

"Listen, gentlemen," I said. "This airplane business is a serious one. I've got two hours to talk Gloria into flying in with me to Home Ranch. I'll make a bet that, if she misses seeing it now, she will never get the chance again."

Maynard turned to Pat.

"Gloria definitely won't do any flying."

"I don't like it too well myself," Pat exclaimed. "I don't trust these crazy airplane motors any more than I do a car engine. Something can always go wrong."

"Here, here," Maynard expostulated. He shrugged and threw his hands above his head. "You don't really mean that, Pat. Why, you're safer in the air with a pilot like Russ Baker in charge than you are working in your own vegetable garden or taking a bath. Insurance companies know that."

"A modern plane," snorted Patterson. "That Junkers is supposed to be one of the two planes of its type left over from World War One."

"That's what the bush pilots all go for," Maynard replied. "One of those old German Junkers'. The safest, most reliable airships ever constructed."

"How about both of you coming along as my guests on the trip?" I asked.

I could see Pat was thinking of some excuse to get out of the air excursion, such as that he had too much work to do, but I also knew he would go to any length to figure out some legitimate excuse to close up shop.

Suddenly, however, Pat's expression changed.

I looked through the window just as Maynard said, "Wowie."

Now the eyes of all three of us swung to a silver-haired, dark-eyed girl who walked down the sidewalk escorted by Sam Cocker and Bob Reid.

For a moment the startling beauty of this young woman took my breath away. Then I recognized her. She was Bob Reid's stepdaughter, Mrs. James Craig, of Peterborough, Ontario.

"Look at that old Cocker," Maynard chuckled. "No woman, married or single, is safe on the streets these days with that Scotsman hanging around."

"I've got an idea," I told the boys.

"So have I," said Pat, quickly stepping out of the door and hailing the threesome.

I moved in behind Pat, and Maynard stood smiling in the doorway.

We all exchanged greetings and Pat said, "Rich is

giving a cocktail party on Russ Baker's Junkers this afternoon and he has invited Mollie Craig along. Not Cocker and not Reid."

"Now look here, Pat," Cocker complained, "I'm chaperoning Mrs. Craig this afternoon, and I wouldn't allow this lovely lady aboard the same plane with the band of you orangoutangs."

"Let's get going, everybody," I snapped. "Time is creeping up on us. Both you gentlemen are invited on this airplane trip, but you, Mollie, are essential. Not only because of your lovely personality, but as a companion to Gloria whom we are planning to shanghai."

Mollie Craig was delighted to go along. Pat, Maynard and Sam accepted. Bob Reid had to go back to his hotel. It was agreed that the gang, with Mollie in the lead, would get as many spiked drinks under Gloria's belt as were necessary to put her in the proper spirit—that is, the spirit of the plane trip. It would not be easy.

The boy still held my saddle horse. I took my bridle reins, stepped across and rode over to the house to tell Gloria innocently that the plane would pick me up at Nulki Lake in a short while. The rest of the party walked up the street towards the liquor store.

I didn't have to wait long. Patterson had somehow got his battered old car running and the gang piled out in front of the house. Gloria was delighted to see Mollie, and the girls talked animatedly while Maynard and Pat poured the drinks—one special one for Gloria. Sam and I served them out on the lawn.

The Bear slunk into a porch corner where he broke into one of his sulky moods. Despite, or probably because of his long association with cowhands, prospectors, trappers and various breeds of men from the bush, the Bear remained a rabid teetotaler. What's more, he was devoid of all humor when it came to the other man and his personal drinking habits.

I usually opened a bottle of beer in the clothes closet or some place where I was not observed by the Bear. But just let him catch me popping the cork of a wine bottle or opening a crock of rye, and the old boy would storm off to a neutral corner in a fit of despair, where he remained to make himself miserable company for all those he usually broke bread with.

"Well—here's to your good health, Gloria," said Mollie, flashing her devastating smile. Mollie downed her rye and water with a flourish.

"And to you, Mollie, here's to you and Jim." Gloria raised her glass and almost gagged as she downed two-thirds of it.

"That's a terrible drink," Gloria sputtered in my direction, wrinkling up her face. "That's awful. You must have mixed it."

"Sorry," I said, "I didn't make it. You're just not used to drinking. It's not too strong is it, Mollie?"

"Something wrong with me," Gloria said. With a super effort she tossed off the rest of her rye and water.

Pat relieved the girls of their glasses and walked through the kitchen door towards the bar.

I pulled out my watch. We had an hour and five minutes to plane time on Nulki Lake, twelve miles away.

Pat returned with the girls' glasses. Cocker finished his drink. He and Maynard retired to the kitchen. Gloria and Mollie followed, both of them talking and sipping their drinks. Gloria was enjoying a specially good laugh over something.

Pat raised his glass.

"Everybody drink to Rich and Russ on their lonely trip. Bottoms up."

I could see Gloria having a rough time of it on her second spiked rye, but it seemed to go down a bit easier than her first one.

"I'm going to fly in with you, Rich." Mollie took my arm.

"I'm going along," said Patterson. "Just in case they need blacksmith work at the Home Ranch. Something might be broke down back there that needs fixing."

"I'll go if Gloria and Sam go, too," Maynard suggested. "What a party we can have on that comfortable plane all to ourselves. I'll pick up meats, relishes and sandwich spreads from the store on our way out, and we will have hors d'oeuvres and martinis served on board."

Gloria started to giggle. "Yes, it would be fun, a cocktail party in the air over Batnuni. Wouldn't that be terrific!"

We piled into Patterson's old wreck and chugged to Maynard's store where various provisions were boxed up and piled into the car.

Russ Baker brought the Junkers in to his usual perfect landing. He slid the pontoons up onto the beach. By now our group was howling with laughter. Russ knew each and every one of us well. He looked the happy group over with a knowing smile.

Maynard was dressed in his white grocery uniform, Pat in his formal blacksmith clothes weighted down with tools. Cocker in an immaculate, pin-striped business suit, and me wearing my usual Levi's, riding boots and Stetson hat. The girls were dressed in smart summer clothes. We were a strange-looking assortment.

There was a bit of confusion loading up the plane. Cocker slipped off the wing and fell with a great splash into Nulki Lake. No one paid any attention to him as he floundered waist-deep in the cold water yelling, "My new suit—my new suit."

Soon we were airborne, the Nulki Hills skimming by beneath us.

I rode up in the co-pilot's seat going over maps with Russ. Although he had landed on Airplane Lake at the Home Ranch several times, Russ wanted to go over the route that stretched beyond us. Green, jungle-covered mountain ranges, deep foam-flecked rivers rushing eastwards towards the Fraser. Wide yellow-green valleys untouched by white man, sparkling island-dotted lakes, sickly yellowish-mauve muskegs shaped like crawling octupuses, narrow conglomerate gorges, great ugly fire-killed land masses, gray and black, and always the dreamy-white sawtooth Coast Range hovering across the western horizon, and finally the mysterious domes and crags of the Itcha and Algak mountains that flanked the Home Ranch on the head-waters of the Blackwater.

It was a brilliant cloudless day. Mountains a hundred miles away loomed up as if seen through a magnifying glass.

The Junkers roared through a gap in the Tatuk Mountains under the shadow of the black-and-brown-stained dome of Iron Mountain. Below us sprawled the bays and coves and twisted forms of Tatuk and Finger lakes.

Suddenly the green valley of Batnuni stood out against the black jackpine forests far to the south of us. I crawled through the pilot's door into the big freight compartment of the Junkers where the cocktail party was in full swing.

Maynard in his spotless white uniform was pouring martinis from a cocktail shaker. Sam Cocker was passing around a platter of hors d'oeuvres. The girls were chatting away. Patterson sat in the middle of the floor, his tools scattered about him, a monkey wrench in one hand. He seemed to be working on something.

I yelled at the group, "What's Patterson working on?"

"The engine," Cocker answered.

Patterson turned away from his concentrated efforts for a moment to bellow at me.

"The motor doesn't sound right. Ask Russ if he's got another engine on board so I can cut this one loose. Tell him I've got all the nuts loose and there's just one small bolt holding it on the plane."

Patterson bent back to his work. Maynard hovered over him with the cocktail shaker.

"Batnuni," I yelled. "There's the old Batnuni, Gloria. It's right below us. Look out the window."

"That's what I thought," called Patterson. "I'll drop this motor down onto the ranch. A dead motor's no good to us up here, but they may be able to use it down on Batnuni."

"I'm not going to look down," Gloria said in a loud voice to overshout the roar of the Junkers' engine. "I don't want to spoil this wonderful party by seeing how far down it is to the trees and the ground."

"We'll be down there pretty quick," yelled Patterson. "Just this one bolt to break loose and we'll be back on the ground again. You won't have to look, Gloria."

Pat paused to toss off his martini and Maynard peered through the window.

"Look, folks, the Fawnies coming up. There's good old Tutii and Fawnie Nose, and old Swannell sticking up there, just as proud as when Rich and Charlie McHenry and I were down there with the pack horses."

"I'm not looking," replied Gloria.

"Tell Russ I need a hammer," roared Patterson. "I broke mine on this nut."

"Give me a big double martini," I yelled in Maynard's ear.

"They're all doubles," called the grocer.

"What fun," giggled Mollie.

"I'm glad you talked me into coming," called Gloria.

Russ stuck his head through the pilot's section and motioned me up forward. Maynard started refilling the cocktail shaker as I got in beside Russ and closed his pilot door on the sky party.

Russ pointed through the forward window. One end of Tsacha Lake was coming into view. The wild glacial-heaved country that reached out in front of the plane was an awe-inspiring sight.

Even at this distance some fifteen air miles away, I could see the great sprawling Home Ranch meadow, the open benches of creeping bunch-grass prairie land flanking the Home Ranch on the northern slopes of the Itchas. This huge open land of meadow and range stood out in sheer naked relief, a shimmering golden color against the black forests surrounding it.

I was gripped in a deep wave of nostalgia for this gigantic grassy world where Pan and I had thrown our ropes down so many years before. I could see the grass-country bench five hundred feet above the Blackwater River, where four creeks came together. East of the confluence of the four creeks I could see other yellowish-green openings.

Once Pan and I had named all of this "The Last Chance Country." Far to the east I could see more creeks and more meadows and endless stretches of swamp reaching back towards the bunch-grass ranges of the Itcha and Algaks.

A tremendous country. An inaccessible world of grass and timber and minerals and solitude, most of it untrodden, unknown by man.

I opened up the pilot's door and yelled into the cabin.

"We're over the Home Ranch meadows, Gloria. Take a look at a great layout."

Now even Gloria looked out of the window. Russ touched me on the shoulder and pointed to a series of tiny black dots on the edge of the yellowish meadow. I nodded my head.

Russ yelled in my ear. "I'm going to buzz the buildings and corrals a couple of rounds, then head back to the lake."

Now the plane started to lose elevation. Down-down-down we went.

Russ winged over on the side and we slid down almost on top of the corral series and the ranch buildings. I held my breath. We roared over the corrals, not thirty feet above hundreds of whitefaces jammed in the big holding corral.

There was sudden wild confusion below us. The fence flattened out in every direction as the wild range cows stampeded. I got a fast glimpse of Pan on a big bay saddle horse on one edge of the cow herd.

His rope was tied onto a calf, possibly a yearling. Russ straightened the plane out and I craned my neck backwards to follow the monumental confusion in the corrals.

Now Russ winged the plane again and we came straight towards what remained of the inside corrals, this time not more than twenty feet below us. Pan's bronc was putting on a real bucking exhibition and Pan was trying to ride him out, the big calf plunging and spinning in the air at the end of the cowboy's rope.

I knew Pan's lariat was tied hard and fast to his saddle horn. He could easily get into bad trouble. I caught a fast glimpse of another rider whose bronc was hitting the sky off to Pan's left. I recognized Les Brewster. He too was having a wild ride.

This time, as Russ leveled the Junkers out, I saw the cattle fanning out over the opening. They were burning a rag towards a distant clump of timber. I could almost hear Pan's cuss words booming out across the range.

I looked at Russ. He had a broad grin on his face. He and Pan were old-time friends, and Russ' demolition of Pan's corrals, the scattering of the herd which had probably taken weeks to round up, corral and sort out, was usual North Country humor.

Russ swung the door open and yelled at the spell-bound group in the back.

"How'd you like the show? A stampede at the end of every Russ Baker trip."

We eased down over Airplane Lake, three miles from the utter chaos and confusion of the Home Ranch deba-cle, and skimmed comfortably down the lake to the rocky roadbed of sorts that led down from the ranch.

The plane drifted peacefully towards shore. With the motor shut off, the silence of the lonely little lake bore into us.

Pat Patterson opened the plane door, and without a change of expression stepped off into three feet of water and waded to shore. He picked up a small log and floated it back to the plane.

"A bridge for you, Cocker," he said, looking seriously at Sam. "Stand on it."

Cocker looked down at his partly dried trousers and with only a slight quiver of his high-bridged nose, stepped down on the floating log, which made a fast roll and Sam joined Pat in the water.

Russ Baker grinned widely. "What a group," he said, shaking his head.

"Have a drink, Russ," Maynard suggested, "you might need it." He handed Russ the cocktail shaker.

"I guess we'll have to wait here an hour or two," Russ meditated. "I'll take just one drink, that's all. Just watch-ing you boys in action has unnerved me. I don't know what you're going to do next."

We were now all out on the plane's wing watching Pat and Sam splashing each other.

In the middle of the fun I heard the distant rattle and bang of an iron-wheeled wagon, and a short time later Pan and his new bride hove into view.

Betty was a tall, cheerful, dark-haired beauty.

Congratulations were hurled back and forth. Pan threatened to shoot up the old Junkers and dismantle it. We transferred the fruits and delicacies from the plane to the wagon. Plans were made for Russ to pick Gloria and me up in a week's time.

Mollie, Pat, Sam, Maynard and Russ crawled back aboard the plane. The engine roared a few moments, then the plane took off down the lake.

A group of incredulous Indians who were seeing one of the first planes of their lives had ridden to the lake shore to stare at this white man's wonder bird. Now they wheeled their ponies about and disappeared in the jackpines.

With Pan at the lines, we were jolted, bounced, pounded and thrown over the rocks towards the Home Ranch.

Over the crash and clang and rattle of the iron-wheeled wagon, Pan called to me in his high nasal voice. "Before those critters stray off too far, friend, we better get on their tails and turn 'em."

Then he meditated a moment. "But then on the other hand, we've got to rig up corrals strong enough to hold 'em. It's not gonna be easy to pound 'em into a corral around here for a piece. You and Russ sure give 'em a hell of a scare."

Knowing Pan so well I realized I was in for some

heavy work for a few days. I would have to replace the log corrals that Tommy Holte and I had cut, skidded out of the bush, and rolled into place many years before.

I barked at Pan. "Why didn't you throw together something new enough and strong enough to hold a bunch of spooky range cows? No wonder those corrals fell apart. I'll bet you haven't changed a log since I put them up fifteen years ago."

Pan snorted. "I should have stayed here at the ranch and showed you and Tommy how to build a real corral instead of takin' those pack horses out to Bella Coola. When I build a corral it lasts a lifetime."

CHAPTER XIII

Home Ranch Revisited

OUR VISIT TO THE HOME RANCH was a pleasant one. Pan put a group of Indians to work on a new corral system, and we gathered up the spooked range cows.

I picked out a top bunch of bred cows with their calves alongside and then drove the future Rimrock cows and calves to the bull pasture where they would be behind fence until they were picked up in November.

With great pride I pointed out to Gloria our saddle and harness shed, the first building with a roof on it put up by the Company. I had been the architect and working crew.

Gloria shook her head when she looked upon this great edifice.

"What were you trying to do, Rich, go surrealistic, or were you on a party?"

She started to laugh, but Pan came to my rescue.

"Rich put that there mansion up in one day. Cut those shakes with an axe, sawed the tops off those six trees with a bucksaw, tacked on the stringer poles, and there we had a shelter for our gear.

"It's not his fault those old trees kept agrowin', some of them faster than the others. No sir, in another few years' time the roof will be sitting up there fifty feet above the ground on those jackpines, and our kids will be makin' a lopsided tree house out of it. The only building in B.C. that's got live trees as corner posts, and a roof that's on a catawampus slant where no rainwater has time to find a hole to leak through."

The old barn was a slightly better building; it was chinked with cow manure and swamp moss. The eighteen-foot-long bunkhouse that I described in detail in *Grass Beyond the Mountains* hadn't budged an inch, was rainproof, and sat soundly but, I thought, rather lonely and forlornly on the edge of the river. The bunkhouse was now an Indian house where Indian workers and visitors made their headquarters.

One bright day Pan and I saddled up horses and struck out across the meadow with Pan and Gloria in the lead. Pan and I wanted Gloria and Betty to see the tremendous improvements we had made years before on the big opening. From one end of the meadow we could look from our horses eastwards to see thirty or more stockyards looming high into the horizon. Lush green turf replaced what had once been eight-foot-high brush, hard-topped hummocks and deep holes. Timothy and clover and patches of reed canary grass and lowland redtop stretched from this end of the meadow for miles ahead of us.

"I never saw so much grass in my life," exclaimed Gloria.

Pan swung his arm in an arc. "One time this wasn't all grass and meadow, Gloria."

He explained how Lester Dorsey and he had constructed

a monstrous harrow to be dragged across the bush and hummocks.

"We built a lookout tower ten feet high on the front of the harrow for the driver's seat," drawled Pan. "The floor of the harrow was made up of twelve-inch axe-squared logs, bolted together. We needed sixty lengths, two feet long each, of one-and-a-half-inch-square iron for the teeth."

"I packed in the teeth and the bolts and the blacksmith coal all the way from Quesnel," I bragged to Betty and Gloria.

"Nearly seven hundred pounds of square iron, two hundred pounds of blacksmith coal, more than a hundred pounds of half-inch bolts, and a flock of sharpened car springs," said Pan.

"It took eight pack horses to bring that stuff in the two hundred miles for Lester Dorsey's harrow," I concluded.

"How did you boys ever sharpen up those big chunks of iron?" Betty asked.

"Sledge hammers," Pan said. "Pine cones, black-smith coal, strong arms, strong backs and weak minds. Rich and me and Lester, Tom Baptiste, Benny Stobie, George Pinchbeck, pounded away all one day and half a night."

"Tell about the hookup," I said to Pan. "When the eighteen horses broke loose on Lester."

"There's the old boy," Pan yelled, pointing up ahead. "There's that old rig that tore up many hundreds of acres where no tractors could have gone."

Both girls did some exclaiming when we reined in our horses beside the weather-grayed old monstrosity sporting the high ladder tower and creaky-looking platform leaning at a rakish angle, like a slanted fedora on its top.

"Horses couldn't have pulled that tremendous thing," Gloria exclaimed. "How many did you use? It doesn't look possible!"

Pan pushed his hat over his face. "We hooked up eighteen the first time; five gentle horses and thirteen broncs that never had a harness on them before.

"Lester climbed up on the driver's tower, holding the two long lines. To get the horses all started at once we had to spook them. We shot off guns and pounded on coal-oil tins."

Pan tilted his hat back on his head. His face turned almost blank. A sad expression filled his grayish eyes.

"That was a terrible deal. The big bunch of horses crashed out of there, tight onto those four-horse double-trees you see there. But some damn fool had pulled out the kingpin that attaches the stretchers to the harrow. There was Lester up there on top of the tower with no chance to stop 'em.

"The whole works parted company with the harrow. Lester threw the lines down at me but I missed. Groups of horses pounded off in every direction. We lost a couple of the best horses the Company ever owned.

"Broke their legs. Funny thing, but two of the big bay five-year-old geldings the Company had just bought from Lester, they piled up in a gully. After I seen what happened to Buck and Blaze, I told George Pinchbeck to put a bullet between their eyes." Pan paused a moment. "Lester went into the house and cried and I guess I weakened a bit too.

"Anyway you can't beat that old Lester Dorsey. He pulled himself together pretty quick and said, 'O.K., men, we ain't plumb licked yet. Run in some more broncs. We're gonna cut the power down to sixteen pullers, two sets of horses, eight abreast, this time,' and that's what Lester done.

"Rich here and his kid brother George and old Pennoyer arrived from Batnuni that evening. Once again Lester got all set on that tower. The gentle horses on the outside, the broncs jumping and twitching around in between them.

"Rich here saw the fireworks explode and the outfit roar out of the meadow into the willow swamp. Where the outfit disappeared, we could see the brush aflyin' off in every direction, and Dorsey hangin' on to the lines and handholt up there on the top of the tower.

"It sure looked like he could never ride that swayin', pitchin' tower—but he did. And he got those horses swung around about a mile up the brush jungle. How, I don't know, but he did, and then he gave 'em all a breather.

"About a ten-minute rest, and he tightens up the lines again, pulls out his six-shooter, yells at the cayuses and shoots into the air, and off they went again acrashin' through the brush, leaving a big wide swath behind 'em.

"After that first start we did some adjustin' to the harrow teeth, added some car springs to act as small plows and put one man to work harnessing horses. We needed thirty-two harness, or sixteen sets.

"One bunch of horses were harnessed and hooked to the harrow first thing in the morning. Then at noon, while Lester grabbed off a cup of coffee and a sandwich, sixteen fresh horses all waitin' with their riggin' on was put in position, and away they went, with less than a half hour between shifts.

"All the big horses on the ranch and the range was broke teams before the summer was out, and bare ground stretched off into the distance where the willow jungle had been before.

"You're lookin' at it now."

We pulled away from the historic old harrow and rode to a narrow creek that flowed across the meadow in a straight line.

"That's the irrigation ditch," I pointed out to the girls. "We rigged up a ditch digger, kind of a Martin ditcher rig made of heavy flat iron and an old grader blade or two. Eight horses pulled that ditcher. They had a tough time of it at first, but in less than a week the ditch was finished and we could put water on this whole upper end of the meadow."

"Old Andy Holte drove the eight-horse ditcher team," Pan explained, "and then he switched to a giant heavy-duty disc made up especially by Massey-Harris for us. It took fourteen horses to pull that disc.

"And," said Pan, "the final operation on this here land was the spruce-tree float and harrow. Three big spruce trees cabled together—a ten-horse job, and the meadow was as level as you see it now.

"Yes sir, this end of the meadow we done the hard way, but it was the horses put her over, and the men who drove them."

Pan wound up his eulogy on horses and meadows.

"I'm just pointing out to you two city-raised girls what horses can do if you got the riggin' and you know how to handle 'em. Ten big horses all lugging together can equal more power than what they call a forty-horse-power tractor. This is one of the last horsepower layouts there is, and these soft-grass B.C. mountain cayuses did the job."

"Look," Betty called, pointing off to our left.

A group of cow moose and calves suddenly shot up out of the grass and headed for the distant timber. Behind them trotted two big bulls who started their roaring chant of anger as they vanished in a low-lying grass-covered ravine.

A short distance farther on, our horses were startled by a big grizzly and two younger ones. The old bear rose up on her hind legs to survey us, and we veered away from them at an angle loping our horses until there was plenty of acreage between the grizzlies and us.

"Just an old sow." Pan grinned at Betty and Gloria. "Lots of 'em around here, but they don't do us or the cows no harm."

"I don't like them," Gloria said.

Betty agreed with Gloria. "I certainly don't like grizzlies, and especially in my back yard."

If Betty had looked into the future she could not have made a more appropriate remark, for she later had an experience with grizzlies that would have left a hardened woodsman with nightmares for the rest of his life.

That week at the Home Ranch brought back old memories, and it was with deep reluctance that I drove down in the wagon to meet the Junkers at Airplane

Lake. Gloria and Betty kept up a steady stream of woman talk in the back of the wagon box. Pan and I remained silent on the front seat. As we jolted across the big meadow I looked about me. I thought of the many experiences Pan and I had had discovering this vast ranch land, and the many happy times, the work and energy we had put into the building and development of this grassy empire.

Now it was quite possible I was looking on our old stomping grounds for the last time.

When we crawled aboard the Junkers, Gloria and I tried to persuade Les Brewster, Pan's top hand, to fly to Vanderhoof with us.

Brewster had a bad case of blood poison in his right hand which was getting worse hour by hour. It was swollen to the size of a small cantaloupe. He was poulticing it with a mixture of home-baked bread and cow manure.

Brewster thought the swelling would go down after Pan lanced it. He said he would ride by saddle horse 140 miles to Bella Coola where there was a doctor if it got much worse.

We waved farewell to the group on the shore. Russ Baker roared the Junkers down the lake and we were airborne over the Home Ranch country. Small herds of deer and moose raced out across the openings. Geese and ducks flapped up and out of the little blue ponds and lakes below us.

"Wonderful country," Frank Coulter, Russ' engineer, called back to us. "Wish I was ten years younger. I'd sure like to go back in here."

"Me too," I yelled, as the plane sped towards the tiny dot of civilization called Vanderhoof, and the miles of little-known wilderness slipped by below us.

Gloria spoke in my ear.

"It's just a perfect shame for somebody with Betty's personality and charm to isolate herself back in that dreary country. The whole time at the ranch I couldn't shake the feeling of loneliness. I know how you and Pan must feel about the country you found and worked so hard on. But somehow the terrible lonely mountains and swamps and jungles must have affected me."

"That's possible," I answered, "but if you lived back there for a while you'd change your mind about that country, I'll bet."

"Never," Gloria said. "I had a strange feeling of uneasiness. I still can't shake it off. No, there's a horrifying ordeal awaiting Pan and Betty. Call it premonition."

"That's a hell of a way to think," I said. "Just like putting the nesachie on the whole gang at Home Ranch."

"I've tried hard to throw off this feeling but I can't," Gloria explained to me.

For a few moments I was almost overwhelmed by various thoughts of what could happen back at the Home Ranch. Then I pulled myself together. Gloria just didn't go for this isolation business. She was like most women who liked people buzzing all around them.

Ever since her Pan Meadow experience when she had her appendicitis attack, and then when Mrs. Hill died, Gloria had been uneasy about the remote bushlands.

When we flew over the high volcanic hills surrounding Rimrock Ranch, Russ called from the pilot's seat.

"I'm going to buzz around over your valley a couple of times. We may see more meadows beyond those timbered benches over there that you people have never seen."

Gloria's face suddenly lost color. She screamed at Russ and Frank.

"Please—please go straight to Nulki Lake and land! Something's going to happen!"

Russ looked at Gloria questioningly, then at me. I winked and nodded towards Nulki. Russ saluted, and turning back to his panel, swung the Junkers toward Nulki Lake.

"What the devil's eating you now?" I barked at Gloria.

"We could have seen the country surrounding Rimrock—and for free. We may never get this chance again. We've been in the air better than an hour now. You've got the spooks again."

"I've had a premonition," she said between clenched teeth. Her face had turned a pale green color.

Fifteen minutes later Russ slipped the old Junkers down onto Nulki Lake. Maynard was there with a flashy new car to meet us. We all drove to town to cocktails and a buffet supper at the Kerrs'.

Early the following morning Maynard, Russ and Frank Coulter took off in the plane on a prospecting trip. They landed on a small lake a few minutes' flying time from Nulki. Maynard and his supplies were put ashore, a date made to meet at the same spot.

The plane took to the air, made a sudden wing over at the end of the little lake and landed back on the water.

The gas line had broken in mid-air spraying gasoline all over Russ and Frank, the pilot's compartment, and more important of all, the open and exposed motor. Russ quickly flopped the plane back on the lake. He said it was a miracle the plane hadn't caught fire and exploded in mid-air, but the engine had not yet become hot.

If we had gone exploring for even ten minutes' time the day before, with the engine red hot from the long trip from the Home Ranch, the plane would have exploded between Rimrock and Nulki.

Gloria's premonition had been right. It was a close call. She could not explain the uncanny warning that suddenly gripped her as we flew over Rimrock Ranch. And don't believe that she hasn't used that experience to her advantage ever since to slow me down on some scheme or adventure I was about to undertake!

"I've had a strange premonition," Gloria says, and that settles the argument.

CHAPTER XIV

Beef to Vancouver

IMMEDIATELY FOLLOWING THE JUNKERS' gas line episode, I did a bit of worrying about my pals at the Home Ranch, but as the months flew by, time and events in my own life gradually obliterated the spooky worry that Gloria's premonition about Pan and Betty had planted in my mind.

That fall an old friend of mine, one of the top cowboys and cow bosses in British Columbia, Bill (Long Loop) Anderson, arrived at Rimrock a few days before I was starting my beef out to the railroad.

I was faced with two big moves at one and the same time. The first was driving out and selling some beef in Vancouver, which was a must as we and the banker needed money in the worst way. And at the same time it was necessary for me to line up a trail crew and ride back 225 miles to the Home Ranch to pick up the cows and calves we were to take over from the Frontier Company.

The Rimrock beef drive and shipment to Vancouver would eat up at least sixteen days. That would bring us into November. Riding back to the Home Ranch, gathering up the cows and calves and trailing them out to Rimrock would take at least forty days—bringing us into the snowstorms and bitter cold of late December.

The only way to put over these two objectives was for me to be in two places at the same time. But when Bill Anderson arrived to visit and to buy a bull calf from us we found he was fancy free for a month, and our problems were solved. Top hand Long Loop Anderson would take over the Home Ranch-to-Rimrock drive, while I took out the beef to Vancouver.

In return for this favor, Rimrock would give Anderson his choice of our bull calves, which to my way of thinking wasn't half enough to pay Bill for what he was to go through.

Short, wiry, bandy-legged Bill Anderson, who had spent his life in the saddle, was adept in every phase of the back-bush cattle game. Bill lined up his crew, his grub and equipment and rigging for the pack string. The crew included Walter Erhorn, Gordon Wilson and young Swede Solmonson.

Bill packed three unbroken mares and four broken trail horses and added several of his own saddle horses to the string. The gang got off to a good start with the unbroken mares hitting the sky. Two of them upended a few yards from the ranchhouse in a ditch filled with muddy water.

After a bit of confusion and a slight delay, we had the cayuses lined out again and the horses and trail crew disappeared around a bend in the road going hell for leather.

I didn't see or hear from the gang for forty-two days. It was late in November when Long Loop Anderson and his trail outfit broke into the Rimrock with the cows and calves without the loss of a single head.

In the meantime, Sam Goodland and our neighbors

Neil Erhorn and Herman Weinhardt threw in with me to land the Vancouver-bound Weinhardt beef and ours at the stockyards of the little town of Fort Fraser, twenty-five miles west of Vanderhoof. It was dark when we eased the cattle across the railroad tracks a mile from the Fort Fraser stockyards.

A fast-moving freight train roared around the bend, the sharp beam of the headlight breaking the darkened tracks and with the whistle wide open. The steers went berserk and stampeded in the direction of town. As I raced Rhino between the engine and the wildly running beef, I could hear the scream of barbwire fences going out above the roar of the freight train.

A mile of fence outside of town was flattened, an odd front porch was knocked for a loop, two old men, a fat boy and old woman were nearly run down in the wild stampede. We spent half the night riding through back yards and garbage dumps, picking up shaken and bewildered cattle, driving them through the darkened streets and into the stockyards.

In the meantime it started to rain. It wasn't long before we were riding around in the night hunched over in our saddles like a bunch of drenched rats. By the time the stock train pulled in, which was about four A.M., we had a count on the herd. It was a miracle that not a single head was missing; in fact we were two head to the good. Believe it or not, we found later the two extra head belonged to Bill (Long Loop) Anderson, whose ranch was at least five days' drive from Fort Fraser.

There are some people who are under the impression that riding the cabooses is a romantic experience. Once I thought this too, but I found out differently. It is an extremely tedious job, particularly so on the long six-hundred-mile run from Fort Fraser to Vancouver. Without a doubt the worst trip I ever got tied up with was this particular one following the stampede on the main street of Fort Fraser.

This trip to Vancouver with the beef turned out to be an ordeal for the cattle and the various trainmen. There were six section points where we changed cabooses and trains, and cars were shuttled and shifted about between Fort Fraser and Vancouver. Something went wrong between each section point. The total trip took nearly six days.

After a great deal of trouble loading the cattle, the train was moving slowly down the tracks when the engineer must have slammed on the brakes or made a false move of some kind. There was a great crashing and grinding of cars ahead of us, then a sudden terrific jar.

The conductor flew off his desk seat, skidded the full length of the car. A lamp crashed to the floor from its holder, and the brakeman and Mr. Bolton of Fort Fraser, who was also shipping cattle, and I lit in a pile near the cursing conductor.

The entire caboose was strewn with papers, loose coats and junk. We struggled to our feet only to be upended again. I kept thinking of the steers and what had happened to them up more than sixty cars ahead of us. At least the jerk and the jar would be far less effective up in front next to the tender than back here at the tail end of the long freight. The conductor was shouting above the din.

"That son of a bitch! That son of a bitch! This is the

last trip, that low-down son of a bitch! I told 'em not to put that guy on again."

During the ninety-mile trip to Prince George we were jolted, banged, and thrown back and forth across the caboose. As we pulled into the yards at Prince George, both the conductor and the brakie literally flew off the rear platform headed for the yard office. This was that engineer's last trip with the C.N.R. all right!

Mr. Bolton and I spent hours with a prod pole, boards and planks, getting trampled steers and heifers to their feet. It was a wonder that none of them were dead. The packing houses that finally bought those beef must have found an awful mass of bruised meat.

In Prince George there was some kind of a mix-up. Our stock cars were sidetracked for eight hours. Mr. Bolton and I wandered around the mile-long length of the railroad yards in the dark looking for our new caboose. Both of us made ourselves unpopular in the yard office trying to get the stock cars hooked to a fast fish train that was supposed to be bound for Vancouver, explaining to various pink-cheeked baby-faced youths behind desks that there was a law saying that cattle had to be unloaded every thirty-two hours for feed and water. Seventy-five-year old pioneer Mr. Bolton, who was due in Vancouver for an operation, picked up a passenger train in the mountains near Red Pass.

We ran into a cloudburst. An avalanche nearly derailed us. There was another long delay.

Late that night our train jolted to a stop. The emergency air brakes took hold, the brakie rushed past the conductor and me grabbing a handful of rocket flare lights as he cleared the rear platform, not losing a step in his run.

The conductor turned pale in that brief instant. He grabbed up two hand lights and ran out of the caboose yelling at me.

"Jump fast, boy—get clear of the tracks. The passenger from Edmonton is less than two minutes behind us!"

His lights disappeared up the track as I broadjumped well clear of the caboose and stumbled over the rocks towards the looming bulk of a cut bank. The distant sound of our train engine, nearly a mile of cars ahead of us, was suddenly drowned out by the rushing roaring noise of the fast passenger rounding the bend behind us, its strong headlight overcoming the line of flares the brakie had been throwing to the track as he made the fastest quarter mile run of his life.

"What an outfit," I kept saying to myself. The scream of the engine brakes nearly split my eardrums. The passenger engine ground to a stop twenty feet behind the caboose.

That night a heavy wet snow stealthily purred down in front of the glaring headlights of the passenger engine. There was monumental excitement among the trainmen and a lot of fast action.

I climbed back on the caboose and listened and watched. Soon I found out what had happened. The old coupling on a carload of baloney bulls had broken, turning our entire freight train loose on the long hill.

Apparently another section was not too far behind the passenger train. Lanterns and flares broke darkness. There were quick conferences between train crews, the bull car was pulled to a siding with giant chains.

In the meanwhile, two freights and another express roared by us on the single track next to our siding.

At Blue River Junction, on the main line, it was necessary to unload the carload of big baloney bulls and shift them on to another stock car.

The ramps and corrals had not been used for years. In the dark of night several of the bulls broke through the rotten-planked old ramp landing in a tangled pile at its bottom.

We lost another six miserable hours getting the panicky old bulls safely on the car. In all the trip took five nights and days to arrive at the Vancouver stockyards. The cattle and I were wrecks when we got there. It was neither pleasant nor romantic.

A few years later Gloria had the brilliant idea of riding a caboose to Vancouver as the caretaker of three cars of cattle. We were shipping five cars of mixed beef from Rimrock and at the time my friend Hutch Hutchinson, our Vanderhoof station agent, the owner of a prodigious sense of humor, made out her caretaker's papers.

A caboose ride appealed to Gloria's sense of glamour and adventure, but she didn't realize then that it was against C.N.R. rules for women to ride the cabooses. The upshot of the episode was that at one of the section points a conductor with little sense of humor and a strong grasp on the little green book of railroad rules got jittery and started to put Gloria off his caboose in the middle of the night at the few lonely cabins of Blue River station.

However, he had no success as there were no policemen in evidence at Blue River, and Gloria continued on to the Vancouver market with her three cars of cattle and me with my two. What with the dirt, the dust, the hard old bench and no sleep for three nights, Gloria never again suggested escorting beef to market.

CHAPTER XV

The Floods

THE TERRIBLE YEARS OF 1947 and 1948 descended upon us with floods, blizzards, icy temperatures and viruses. Atom bombs were exploding and, we were told, apparently changing the pattern of climates.

It was July of 1947. We were haying on the Rimrock meadows when we heard the hum of a car coming down onto the valley floor. Earl Dahl drove his taxi through the gates. He carried a telegram from Gloria's brother in Vancouver. Aunt Kate was very ill. Gloria hurriedly threw some clothes into a suitcase and headed back to town with Earl to catch the train for Vancouver.

Late in the afternoon of the day she left I noticed ominous black clouds piling up above the distant Nulki Hills. We continued haying in a horrifying cloud of man-eating black flies and mosquitoes.

Suddenly it grew very black—almost like night. A blinding flash lit up the whole land. Several more terrific flashes followed, and then came crash after crash of thunder, the like of which I had never heard before. We headed at a run for the ranchhouse, but before we reached it a terrific cloudburst broke loose overhead. The force of the cascade of rainwater that poured down almost knocked us to the ground. Off behind the fences I heard the pounding of many hoofs as cattle and horses stampeded into the bush.

We crowded through the doors of the ranchhouse in the semi-darkness, drenching the floors with water pouring from our boots and clothes.

Most cloudbursts let up after a few violent minutes but this one didn't slow down one bit. All around us and off towards the Nulki Hills breathtaking flashes of lightning lit up the dark green atmosphere and the drenching blankets of water crashing earthwards. The roar of the storm and the staccato of rain on the roof compelled us to yell instead of speak inside the house.

Clothes were hung up to dry around the kitchen stove and the two heaters. Teams, saddle horses and our two milk cows stabled, chores completed, supper eaten, the crew retired to the crash of thunder and torrential pounding of rain. All during that strange eerie night I tossed around in my bed and worried about what the storm would do to our stock and the hay we had sweatingly put up in the stack. I thought about the crew.

There was Jack Lee, who had just ridden in from Batnuni to help us for three weeks with the haying, Walter Erhorn, and the Helland family who lived in the bunkhouse three hundred yards from the main ranchhouse. Al Helland was an average-sized man of about thirty years of age who had one leg shorter than the other, resulting in a noticeable limp. And there was Mrs. Exeter, our neat, well-educated but slightly confused cook. Mrs. Exeter was a quiet dark-haired woman who was as deaf as a post and who had apparently encountered nothing but hard luck in the last ten years of her life. She had lost two husbands in five years and had taken to alcohol to blur out her unhappy memories. After her rare trips to town she would arrive back at the ranch, rather tipsy and slightly disheveled, carrying several bottles of rum for her tapering-off process.

Besides being an excellent cook Mrs. Exeter was a perfectionist at making home-brew beer, but there were only a few times that we were able to taste the finished product. She had a habit of drinking up the liquid while it was still in the bubbling mash stage and covering up by adding water to the bottled result.

The storm noises seemed to subside shortly before daylight and I fell asleep. In my restless slumber I was conscious of a different sound from the wild storm and I came to with a start. The rain had eased off to a steady purr on the roof, but what caught my ear was the washing, gurgling roar of water around the house. It sounded like a ship plowing through heavy seas. I rolled quickly out of bed and stepped to the window.

For a moment the sight that greeted the eye made me think I was dreaming. Our ranchhouse was standing alone and aloof, hardly a foot above a vast muddy torrent of rushing water. On all sides of the house and reaching in every direction, as far as the eye could see, this flowing lake with uprooted trees, fence posts and enormous rolling piles of brush and hay swept by. You could not tell where the road was. Six feet of churning brown water swept between the house and the Rimrock side hill.

The bridge between the ranchhouse and the barns was submerged and only the stables and several manure piles with calves perched on their tops stood above the moving water that reached off into the distance. It was a frightening sight. I had seen floods before. Even this year's spring flood had been destructive enough. Walter and I had spent nearly two months setting new fences and cleaning up the mess in its wake, but never before had I seen anything like this. Unless you have gone through such a flood you have no idea of the terror and panic that it creates in even a normally adjusted person.

I jumped into my pants and ran into the main part of the house yelling,

"Boots and saddles! We're getting swept away in a flood!"

Jack Lee and Walter sprang from their beds reaching for their trousers as they hit the floor.

"Look—look out there!" gasped Jack when he reached the window. "Where the hell are the horses?"

"The milk cows!" yelled Walter. "They're marooned in the barn. What about the Hellands and their kids up in the bunkhouse?"

I had pulled myself together enough for my meager brain to start clicking. Mrs. Exeter walked sleepily out of her room into the living room rubbing her eyes. She saw us staring unbelievably out the windows.

"What's happened?" she exclaimed.

When she glimpsed the rampaging waters outside the windows she began chanting, "Oh my God, oh my God. I knew it—I knew it. Everywhere I go something terrible happens. Now it's my turn, my turn, it's the end."

Walter said, "Where's the boat? What the devil did we do with that boat?"

"Throw some pancakes and bacon on the stove," I bellowed at deaf Mrs. Exeter. "It's not as bad as it looks."

Suddenly Jack exclaimed,

"Look, boys, here comes Al Helland in the boat. He's floating right over the top of the corral."

Mrs. Exeter was staring spellbound at Helland as he rowed smartly up to the front door in our tiny plywood dinghy.

"Was I drinking last night?" moaned Mrs. Exeter. "I think I have the D.T.'s." She held her head between her hands and swayed back and forth.

We all walked to the front door where Helland had tied the dinghy to the doorstep.

"You're high and dry here." Al Helland grinned. He pulled out a ruler and measured the distance between the floodwater and the floor of the porch.

"Eight inches," he said, shrugging. "Lots of leeway."

Helland slopped through the door into the kitchen where he shook himself like a Saint Bernard dog.

"Had to swim over to where we had the boat," he commented.

"Please," said Mrs. Exeter. "Please go in another room, boys. I'm all mixed up and I want to cook you some breakfast."

Walter said, "Let's get those doggie calves off the manure piles and into the house before they fall in and drown."

"We've got to milk those cows," said Jack, "and swim them over to the side hill before they drown in the barn."

Al Helland, who obviously was a water man, rowed us in relays over to the barn where we all went to work. We hogtied the three doggie calves we were caring for and heaved them into the boat. One at a time Helland rowed them to the ranchhouse where he turned them loose in the kitchen. I had told him to drag them onto the glass-enclosed porch, but he forgot. The calves bucked and played about the kitchen. He told us that Mrs. Exeter kept holding her head and chanting, "Oh my God. Oh my God. What has happened to my mind? What has happened?"

Al then rowed the two milk cows' calves some distance beyond the ranchhouse to the Rimrock side hill where he held them while they bawled for their mothers. There was six inches of water in the barn. We led the milk cows out of the barn door where they picked up the cries of their calves. Jack Lee jerked off their halters and the old girls plunged into the cold swim and struck out for the side hill.

Now we were faced with the problem of what to do with the wrangle mare who was also tied up in the barn.

"Front porch," I told the boys. "We'll boat some hay over to her. Emergency, you know. Mrs. Exeter will just have to understand. We'll clean up the mess if the ranchhouse doesn't get washed away in the froth. There's one thing for sure. We're not going to be left afoot."

After considerable difficulty we managed to swim the wrangle mare to the front door and led her into the porch where Mrs. Exeter greeted us with bugged eyes and many shakings of head and gaspings of "Oh my God, oh my God." "I saw two bloated cows float past," she wailed, "the poor creatures. The poor creatures. Why should God take out His wrath on these poor innocent creatures?"

"I saw them," Al said. "Lord knows how many more of this outfit's cattle are gone. But there's just nothing we can do about it all."

Mrs. Exeter stared at the slightly dazed mare.

"Poor little creature," she said. "Poor little creature." She reached out and stroked the wet neck of the mare. There was a sudden crash in the kitchen and the sound of falling dishes. Jack Lee and Walter came bounding through the living room in the wake of the happy calves, one of whom slammed into Mrs. Exeter, upending her onto the couch. The wrangle mare bolted and the whole outfit, all but Mrs. Exeter, ended up in wild confusion on the glassed-in porch. We closed the door on the frightened livestock.

Helland rowed to the barn and returned with a boatful of hay which he scattered about the porch. He informed me that the bunkhouse where his wife and two children were ensconced was still a foot and a half above the floodwaters. He didn't seem the slightest bit worried; in fact we were all beginning to get into the spirit of the thing. Helland rowed off over the corrals towards the bunkhouse.

I knew only too well that Rimrock Ranch and its livestock had had the business even if the ranchhouse and bunkhouse weren't carried away, and that our winter's hay for the stock was gone. Financially we were already in a precarious position and now it looked as if Gloria and I were ruined. What we were going to do in the immediate future faced me with such an overwhelming force that I dared not look ahead more than twenty-four hours at a time. I was thankful for one thing though—that

Gloria was not here to see the devastation of Rimrock Ranch and our meager fortunes.

The following morning the rain let up. The sun peeked miserably through the vanishing clouds on a vast haze of steam rising up from the muddy flowing waters that reached across the valley from bank to bank. Now only the lap of flowing water could be heard and the anguished bawls of distant cows calling in vain for their calves.

The water was still rising. It lapped against the top of the front step. Two more inches and it would be in the house. It was at this stage of the flood that I witnessed one of the most remarkable rescue feats I have ever seen or heard of.

The Queen, our Saint Bernard, had died the previous summer and Gloria and I had replaced her with a half Saint Bernard-half police dog yearling whom we named Uncle Boswell. My brother George, who had returned from the war, presented us with a registered German Shepherd bitch whom I called Pup-Pup-Pup. True to her name the Pup-Pup-Pup quickly produced four pup-pup-pups at Rimrock and since the flood had been nursing them on the bed in my room. The old Bear got along amazingly well with Uncle Boswell and his family.

We had also adopted a tiny three-legged tortoise-shell female cat whom we called Wee Trapper, and a chunky little stray tomcat whom I found asleep in George Ogston's Scotch golf cap in the realtor's Vanderhoof office. Mr. Ogston happily presented me with his little protégé who had been following him all over town. I named the gray tom for his mentor—George—but I added "Little" to his name. Little George was later to become quite a famous tomcat, but at the time of the flood his only claim to fame was that he had sired eight kittens by the Wee Trapper. The Wee Trapper had shacked up across the bridge near the barn in the calf shed which went under water the second day of the flood.

The boys and I were sitting silently in the living room a short time after breakfast when I heard the old Bear barking from the porch steps where we had thrown together a makeshift boat-landing platform. Mrs. Exeter ran excitedly from the kitchen into the living room.

"Quick, everybody! Quick! Look out the window. Oh my God, oh my God, he'll never make it. Somebody do something!"

As I gathered my shattered nerves together for the usual leap to the window, I started saying to myself, "Oh my God, oh my God."

We all reached the window at the same time. We saw Boswell swimming hard against the current. He carried something in his mouth. He made the main channel by the bridge and then swam easily up to the porch to gingerly deposit his tiny burden. It was one of the Wee Trapper's kittens and the little thing was alive.

Uncle Boswell dove back in the water and swam towards the submerged calf shed. A short time later he swam across the channel with another kitten. He looked at it sadly for a moment after he dropped it on the platform. The poor little kitten was dead.

One by one Boswell swam six of the tiny kittens across the channel. Three of them lived. Later the dripping-wet Wee Trapper was purring over her three remaining offspring. Whether or not Boswell had swum her across we will never know, but I wouldn't be at all surprised if he did for I doubt very much if the little cat could have navigated the swift current with her three legs.

Now the main ranchhouse looked and smelled like a zoo. It housed three dogs, four puppies, two cats, three kittens, three doggie calves, the wrangle mare and our heterogeneous group of humans.

Late in the afternoon we heard someone yelling on the side hill. Looking through my binoculars I saw our neighbor, Herman Weinhardt. He was down from his ranch on the bench three miles away to see how we were faring and if there was any way he could help us. Herman got wet to his shoulders covering the distance from the top rail of the fence to the porch door. While he was drying out his clothes I persuaded Mrs. Exeter, with loud yells and sign language, to produce a case of unwatered home-brew beer, which she finally uncovered beneath a number of cases of her bottle bilge water.

We retired with the beer to the porch to join the livestock and watch night descend on the floodwaters. The water had stopped rising just in time. Nearly a half inch covered the porch floor, but it had remained stationary for several hours. The pale yellowish sunset faded into the descending darkness and all we could hear was the murmur of the flood and the slap-slap-slap of it as small waves splashed against the house foundation. Occasionally a floating tree or pile of willows tangled up with hay would lodge against the house or barn or calf shed, causing a gurgling roar and hollow suction noise, to break the monotony of the hushed advance of the muddy water.

Suddenly the Bear and Uncle Boswell broke loose in a crescendo of excited barks and yowls. Al Helland had the boat up at his bunkhouse and Herman Weinhardt was just steeling himself for the cold wet plunge to reach the top rail of the corral fence where it jutted out of the water near the side hill, when we could distinctly hear the distant noise of a car or truck descending the hill. A few moments later the headlights of the vehicle pierced the darkness far up the flooded valley.

"Look at that," I exclaimed to the boys. "That car better stop right now. There's at least six feet of water at the big rock just in front of them."

"The damn fools," cracked Walter. "Look—they're driving straight into the drop-off."

The bunch of us stood spellbound along the porch windows watching the lights of the doomed vehicle approach the point of no return—and then it happened— there was a distant splash. Lights and cab disappeared beneath the muddy water. Jack, Walter, Herman and I were so absorbed and fascinated by the catastrophe up the valley that we had not heard the living room door open, nor were we conscious of Mrs. Exeter breathing down our shoulders. She had arrived among the live-stock and ourselves in time to see the disappearance of lights and car.

"Oh my God, oh my God," she kept saying. "Oh my God. Just like when my husband drowned. Somebody go to their help! Somebody go to their help—people are drowning out there!"

"It's their own damn fault," retorted Jack Lee. "Any fool could have seen they was driving into a lake."

Now yells and curses drifted down to us from the side hill.

Herman said, "I guess I may as well swim for the fence now as ever." He pulled his big straw hat down hard on his head, opened the porch door and with a hollow splash entered the chilling waters of Rimrock. Walter and Jack ran into the living room and returned with two lanterns glowing.

We could see Herman astraddle the top corral log above the water, shinnying his way towards the side hill. And then on the bottom of the hill the dark figures of two men appeared.

"Hello, this place!" one of them yelled. I recognized my brother George's voice. "What's the name of this lake? It's not on the map."

Herman reached the hill and I could see him sitting on the fence shaking hands with the other man who had managed to splash up onto the rail.

I said, "What the hell," settled my Stetson on my head and entered the water to swim out and greet our guests.

I pulled myself out of the water and clung to the fence as brother George introduced me to the stranger.

"Shake hands with Ernie Pinkham," George said. "Up from Vancouver for a change of scene and a rest cure at Rimrock Lake."

I reached up out of the water to grasp the man's hand. It was too dark to see his face but his handshake was firm and his laugh infectious.

George barked at me, "Gloria's brothers sent Ernie up to relax at the ranch. They weren't able to get word to you because of the washouts between here and Vanderhoof—so I brought him out in my jeep."

Ernie propelled himself a few feet further along the fence. After some confusion we were able to guide the boys through the water to the porch and tote Ernie's water-soaked luggage safely into the living room.

Brother George, with a swift movement like drawing his six-shooter, came up with an unopened bottle of whiskey. He looked first at the bottle and then at Mrs. Exeter with whom he was quite well acquainted.

Mrs. Exeter kept shaking her head and repeating, "Oh my God, oh my God. I thought those poor people out there would all be drowned, just like my husband was. He fell off the boat with high boots on. I guess they filled up with water and pulled him under. I watched him sink. There was nothing I could do. Down he went—not more than six feet from the boat. I'll never forget the look in his eyes as he disappeared forever."

"Open that bottle," I told my brother.

Now in the lamplight I could see Ernie Pinkham, a former Canadian football player and star athlete from McGill University. He was a dark-haired, square-jawed man, now probably in his early forties, well over six feet in height, who still moved like an athlete. His deep-set black eyes showed kindness and tolerance. I noticed that he looked tired, as if he had been under a strain of some kind. I took an immediate liking to him.

As we entered the living room and headed for the heater Ernie suddenly swung about and yelled at George.

"Bob Birch! What happened to Bob Birch. I haven't seen him since we went into the lake."

"Quick," exclaimed George. "Somebody grab a rope. We forgot all about Bob. He was sitting in the back of the jeep when we plowed into the lake."

"What's that?" cried Mrs. Exeter. "What's that? Somebody missing?"

"Easy—" I hollered at her. "Easy, Mrs. Exeter. We're going out on a search party right now."

"Oh my God. Oh my God," moaned Mrs. Exeter, clasping her hands together and swaying from side to side. "I knew somebody was going to be drowned— just like my husband. I saw him go under right before my eyes."

Walter found a long chunk of soft rope and Jack unfastened his lariat from the rope strap on his saddle. We all rushed for the door.

"A silly thing to do," gasped Ernie. "Forget all about the third man in the party."

"He's a good swimmer," George called over his shoulder. "He wouldn't have gotten hurt just sitting there when we went under. But what a hell of a thing to forget he was there."

With Ernie and George in the lead, the rest of us carrying lanterns and ropes and axes behind, we were just splashing into the water when we heard yells and laughs and the creak of oarlocks, and then Al Helland rowed into the lanternlight with Bob Birch, wet and dripping, holding down the rear seat of the boat.

It seems that when the jeep plunged under the water, Bob, finding himself afloat, yelled at George and Ernie that he was going to swim over to the bunkhouse where he knew his cousin, Al Helland's wife, was living. But George and Ernie were so busy sloshing about in the submerged jeep looking for Ernie's luggage that they didn't hear Bob's farewell as he swam over the top of the fence and over-handed towards the light in the distant bunkhouse window.

George stayed over a few days until the flood sub-sided and we were able at last to attach block and tackle to his jeep. While we were pulling the water-logged vehicle to dry land George and Ernie reminisced about their jolly entrance to our peaceful Rimrock Ranch. It seems that at the gap between the rimrocked hills, George stopped the jeep and the three men went to work on a bottle of Scotch whiskey. As the jeep plunged down the steep narrow road, Bob Birch sat quietly in the back while George carried on a rambling discourse about the wonderful valley, the terrific grass, the intelli-gent animals, the peaceful atmosphere that engulfed the magnificent grasslands of Rimrock.

Suddenly Ernie saw the glint of water ahead. He interrupted my brother to say that it looked to him as if they were approaching water. George paid no attention to Ernie's warning and proceeded on with his driving and his eulogies of Rimrock. Finally, in desperation, Ernie yelled at George.

"Stop, George! Put on the brakes! We're driving into a lake!"

"Lake, hell!" retorted my happy brother. "I was here three weeks ago. This isn't any lake. This is a cattle ranch."

And then as Ernie opened the door of the jeep, the outfit plunged into the drink.

I grew to know Ernie Pinkham well. He became fast friends with me and the other members of the Rimrock

crew. Ernie told me that for some time before he had
come north he had felt he was on the verge of a crack-up.
He had been unable to sleep, and worried constantly,
and there just hadn't been any way he could relax. A trip
to a luxurious fishing camp had done nothing for his
frayed nerves.

Now, of all places, to wind up at the zoo house at
Rimrock was an ironic stroke of fate, and I felt at first
that this would be a catastrophe for Ernie, but strangely
enough, as he joined the other boys and me in the various
rehabilitation jobs around the ranch, Ernie began to eat
like a horse, sleep nights and put on weight.

After the flood subsided, the bunch of us cleaned up
the main mess around the yard and helped Mrs. Exeter
turn the zoo back into a house, but the year's haying
operation at Rimrock was over. A heavy layer of gray silt
covered the grass from one end of the valley to the other.
I finally decided to move our outfit down to the Nechako
River fifteen miles away, where Gloria and I had made a
small down payment on an undeveloped ranch layout to
a pioneer trapper named Tom Taerum. I estimated we
could put up 150 to 200 tons of hay down there which
would go quite far in wintering our three hundred head
of cows.

I enlisted the help of Herman Weinhardt and his
iron-wheeled wagon. With our old wagon and Herman's
I figured we would be able to transfer machinery and
equipment to the new hay camp on the Nechako River.

On the appointed day I heard the Weinhardt wagon
rattling and banging down the valley. There was still a
small muddy stream about a foot deep flowing along the

roadbed as he drove his wagon with his three children in the box to the back door.

Then it happened—with a great splash, team, wagon, Weinhardt and children all dropped out of sight.

Pinkham rushed out of the door to the rescue with Mrs. Exeter on his heels. She was screaming, "Just like my husband."

I found myself standing high and dry on the back door step, watching Ernie and Mrs. Exeter running into the washed-out roadbed, yelling, "Oh my God. Oh my God."

Our panic was unnecessary for Weinhardt performed an expert job maneuvering his waterlogged team and wagon up and out of the eight-foot-deep washout on the back road. The kids came up dripping and laughing, still on the wagon box, having lost nothing but their hats which Mrs. Exeter and Ernie floated back to the porch.

We rounded up the cattle and horses and found, much to our surprise, that losses were small. In all we were only out eight head of mixed cows, calves and heifers.

Our fifteen-mile move to the river was successfully negotiated with wagonloads of cats, pups, machinery, provisions, bedding and haying equipment.

Towards the end of the river-haying operation Ernie, who had put on some thirty pounds of muscle and was feeling better than he had for years, said,

"Rich, why don't you gather up your beef now and take them to Vancouver? I'll carry on for you here at the ranch. It's you that's on the verge of a crack-up now. I'll make a bet that a few weeks in the big city will do you as much good as the ranch visit has done for me. You need a change of scenery—and right now."

I followed Ernie's advice. We rounded up the cattle, cut out the cull cows and the beef, enough to make up three carloads, and drove them to the railroad yards at Fort Fraser.

Four sleepless days and nights later I stepped off the caboose at the Vancouver stockyards to be greeted by Gloria and her brothers, Fraser and Jack. We drove to Jack's Cambie Street apartment where Gloria and Jack were living while Aunt Kate was recuperating at a friend's house not far away.

At the Cambie Street apartment Jack would leave for work at eight o'clock in the morning. Gloria would go about her job of cleaning up the dishes, shopping, cooking and visiting her mother, while I sat in a chair with my feet sticking out of the window, staring in silence down at the traffic and the crowds of people on the street below. In the evening we would go to a movie or occasionally dine out. I went through two weeks of this ritual before I began to feel like my old self again.

Our cows and beef brought a good price that year— we sold the lot—and then Gloria and I were on the train shuttling towards the North Country and the long winter that lay ahead of us.

I arrived at Rimrock rested and ready to tackle the new problems that faced us, and Ernie left for his office in Vancouver to resume his business with enthusiasm after his restful visit to Rimrock Ranch.

CHAPTER XVI

The Blizzards

THE NEVER-TO-BE-FORGOTTEN winter of 1947-48 roared down on us suddenly and unexpectedly. We barely had time to round up all the cattle and fence the few hay-stacks that the flood had not washed away when freezing winds swept down out of the Arctic. Fine powdery snow whirled and drifted against the cabin walls. The cattle bawled and the horses pawed into the white mantle that covered the ground.

This was late in October but a month and a half before we usually had to feed hay to the stock. I knew we didn't have nearly enough to last the hungry cattle through the long winter that lay ahead.

Walter's brother, Neil Erhorn, and Sam Goodland were working for us. The other boys had already returned to their own ranches for the winter.

There was only one thing for us to do—buy hay wherever we could at the closest ranches and move the cattle to the feed.

I saddled up and, leading a pack horse, rode out into the storm in search of hay. I lined up several stacks at the Erhorn ranch ten miles away. Then at a lonely forlorn swamp meadow eighteen miles beyond Rimrock called

Martin Lake I was lucky enough to locate another fifty tons from Newt Dawson, an old-timer who once had owned the upper end of Rimrock Valley. In the opposite direction, some twenty miles from the ranch at the old Blair meadow I bought forty tons of good timothy.

Back at the valley I told Gloria and the two boys of the plan I had been working on. If we followed it out I was certain we could pull all the stock through no matter what kind of winter lay ahead.

We would leave the weaned calves and weaker cows at Rimrock and drive all the strong stuff out to the hay. I had had the good fortune of hiring a young rancher named Bob Morris to stay with the stock and take care of them. If the outside hay held up until the middle of January we would be set, for by then there would be enough hay left at Rimrock to carry the outfit through to March when we would move everything down to the Nechako River ranch where with the help of Ernie we had stacked up the 150 tons. This would see the stock through to green-grass time.

From that day it seemed that we were always on the trail, stiff and numb with cold, driving the cattle and horses into a frozen white world. There never seemed to be any let-up from the bone-chilling winds, the blasting clouds of snow and temperatures that often dropped to more than fifty below zero. But the cattle and horses were fed all they could eat and stayed up in shape.

When we moved the stock from one hay camp to another it was necessary to drive a bunch of horses ahead of the cattle to break trail through three or more feet of snow. At last, towards the middle of January and on the planned schedule, we plunged the stock through the drifts back to Rimrock Valley.

Our troubles were now really to begin. Our resistance to the cold blasts had played out. We were sick men. All of us had coughs. Bob Morris seemed to be on the verge of pneumonia. I made him saddle up his horse and ride through the drifts to town and a doctor. A few days later Sam Goodland's cough weakened him so much that he could barely get out of bed. Neil Erhorn and I rigged up a plank V snowplow and pulled it with a team of horses as far as Weinhardt's and the plateau road, where the drifts weren't as bad and the snow not so deep. Then I sent Sam towards the Vanderhoof hospital in our Jeep. I knew he had picked up a thriving case of pneumonia. We didn't see him again for a month and a half.

Sam and Bob cleared out of the valley just in time. Soon after their departure the record cold snap of central British Columbia bore down on us. From the twentieth of January to the twenty-fourth of February the mercury hovered between thirty and seventy degrees below zero. The longest and coldest period in the history of the north.

At Rimrock it was necessary for Gloria to tape Neil Erhorn's eyes open with adhesive tape so that he could see to drive the feed team. His face had bloated badly, closing both eyes. He had virus pneumonia but he wouldn't give up. My own lungs, chest, abdomen, ached with the pain of coughing.

Then a terrific Arctic blizzard crashed down from the north. Drifts of fine powdery snow piled high upon the already snow-crusted land. Rimrock was completely isolated from the outside world.

Ten miles from Rimrock at the Erhorn ranch, tragedy hit hard. Bob Erhorn, Walter's and Neil's brother,
lay for weeks in the Vanderhoof hospital hovering
between life and death. In a room next to Bob's, the old
pioneer Billy Erhorn, their father, passed away in a fit of
coughing. Mrs. Erhorn, like her eldest son, Bob, was
close to the edge for many weeks.

Doctor Alvin Mooney, farm-raised medical genius of
the North Country, and the nurses and dedicated sisters
performed miracles in the St. John Hospital pulling the
ranchers and farmers and townspeople of this stricken
country up and out of the plague of virus that had landed
upon us.

As we struggled against the odds and the strange quirks
of nature, Gloria and I often talked and thought about Pan
and Betty and their children in the land of the Blackwater,
that remotest of all ranches in North America. How were
they surviving the storms, the blizzards and the cold?

Then one day while I was feeding cattle in long
snowdrifted runways far out on the meadow, I saw Rhino
with Gloria in the saddle, plunging through the drifts
towards my feed team. I knew something had happened.

I tried to look nonchalant as I rolled a large chunk of
frozen hay off the sleigh. Gloria jerked off the silk scarf
that she had wrapped over her nose and cheeks. Her breath
spurted out in a tiny wreath of blue steam.

"I just had to get the news out to you, Rich. Something
terrible must have happened to Pan. A message just came
over the Prince George radio for Betty Phillips at Home
Ranch. The announcer just repeated twice: 'Pan Phillips
resting comfortably in hospital.'"

I looked off towards the snow-choked Rimrock pass.

"There's not one thing we can do right now, Gloria, except keep the cattle and ourselves alive until we can get some help in here. No sign of Sam Goodland for a month. Neil in bad shape. Temperature sixty-five below last night, forty below when I left the barn."

Neil came riding up out of the pale white gloom. He packed a newborn calf across his saddle swell. It was as stiff as a plank. Neil coughed, then spoke through the scarf tied over his face and nose.

"The deep freeze got the little devil just as he hit the ground. I can't hear his heart beating, but who can tell— he might live. Anyway I'll take him into the ranchhouse." (The calf lived.)

Neil and Gloria swung their horses about and rode towards the distant ranch buildings. Gloria called back over her shoulder.

"It's frightful! I only wish we could do something. Poor Betty—those little children—two hundred miles of snowdrifts from nowhere."

She had tied her face scarf back on again. Only her eyes showed beneath her parka.

Lordy, I thought. If we think we're having trouble, what about the Home Ranch? What happened back there?

The frost dug into my clothes. I watched Gloria and Neil with the frosted newborn calf ride down the sleigh tracks. Sweat was freezing now between my heavy wool underwear and shirt.

There were two more loads of hay to dig out of the stacks, throw on the sleigh, tote to the spruce grove and throw off to the cattle. Neil and I had already given the critters their daily spook—one of the many little tricks that are necessary to bring a herd of cattle through a prolonged cold snap.

Cows will stand in their tracks, ice-covered backs humped against the cold, for hours at a time. Circulation slows down. Appetites fall off. Hoofs and tails and ears freeze. But a sudden rush on the torpid critters with a saddle horse while beating a tin can starts the herd jumping and bucking off through the snow. Backs limber up and circulation returns.

Every few hours the long narrow trenches in the ice serving as water holes have to be smashed open. Ranchers must work through the short hours of daylight and long into the shimmering starlit nights to bring the cattle through.

It was inky dark and the strange green and white flashes of the aurora borealis were streaking across the sky when I drove the frosted team through the last gate and into the barnyard.

During that long prolonged crisis at Rimrock, Gloria's and my minds often drifted across the lonely mountain ranges to Betty and the little Phillips children. How had Pan been able to get out two hundred miles or more to a doctor if he was seriously hurt?

But the answer to the questions that came to our minds were not to be answered for months to come, and then we were to hear one of the most dramatic and unbelievable stories ever to come out of the interior of British Columbia.

Our outfit survived that terrible winter, and early in March Neil, Sam Goodland and I moved all the stock to the River Ranch while Herman Weinhardt drove the sleigh which contained Gloria, assorted cats, kittens, puppies, provisions and other equipment. The Bear, Boswell and the Pup-Pup-Pup followed behind.

Unbelievably, we had lost only one cow that long tough winter and the rest of the herd were in fairly strong shape. No wonder I am an enthusiastic supporter of Hereford cattle.

CHAPTER XVII

Ordeal on the Frontier

BACK AT THE HOME RANCH, two hundred miles beyond the nearest village, on that ferocious deep freeze winter of 1947-48, the terrific Arctic blizzard suddenly swirled and swished into the tall, wide-branched, blue and silver spruce trees that crowded protectively like dark guardians about the log, shake-roofed ranchhouse and the nearby outbuildings.

The Home Ranch household consisted of Pan and Betty; Willie, Betty's six-year-old son by a previous marriage; Betty and Pan's infant daughter, Diana; and Shag Thompson, a sturdily built, mature, fifteen-year-old hired hand.

Soon the white curtain of the Arctic blizzard blacked out all objects for a distance of two horse lengths.

Pan was feeding hay to the main bunch of grown stock some three miles up-meadow from the buildings in a grove of spruce trees where there was good shelter from the wind. A creek twisted through the tall evergreens providing the necessary water. A series of haystacks bordered the grove.

Every morning at daybreak Pan would harness his team, drive out to the cattle, feed them several loads of hay and open up the water holes. Back at the ranch Shag Thompson fed the bulls, the calves and the hospital bunch, which was made up of any cripples or weak stock.

The day the blizzard hit the northland Shag and little Willie carried on with their respective ranch duties in the usual manner, but when Pan arrived at the feeding grounds three miles from the ranchhouse, he found a two-year-old heifer hamstrung and half eaten by wolves. On Pan's return trip the snow was blowing so thick and the wind behind the pall of white gloom was so fierce that only occasionally could he see the heads and shoulders of the team. Back at the house, an hour late, his high-bridged nose and cheekbones were marble white and one hand was frosted through his mitten. Betty, using a rag dipped in coal oil and some brisk rubbing, brought back his circulation.

On the third day of the storm Pan was unable to buck his team and sleigh through the huge drifts that separated the ranch corrals from the cattle. The only way he could get to the herd of cows at the spruce grove would be to saddle up a strong horse, take a roundabout route around the worst of the snowdrifts and plunge through the rest of them to the stackyards. There he would throw the hay over the fence to the cattle, open up the water holes and set several wolf traps around the carcass of the dead heifer, for there was a good chance that the wolves might come back to feed on their kill.

Pan picked Wang Leather for the job, a 1,300-pound, short-coupled black stallion. Wang Leather was half Percheron and half Thoroughbred, a six-year-old power-house in action whom Pan had only ridden three times, once in the breaking corral, and twice in the open meadow after the first heavy snowstorms of the season.

Betty knew that Pan had ridden Wang Leather on the three previous occasions, that Pan was in perfect condition, that he had been breaking out colts all fall and winter. She also knew that he took chances when he shouldn't. She tried to talk him out of riding the big stallion on this forty-below-zero day, pointed out the risk he was taking, and what it would mean to them all if he got hurt with little or no chance of getting out to a doctor or help. But Pan just grinned and made his customary answer to such talk.

"Hell, Betty," he said. "There's just nothin' to it at all. Everything's easy. There never was a better time to give Wang Leather a workout. He'll be plumb broke and gentle when he gets back out of those snowdrifts. Besides, I don't figure we got another horse in the yard that could break trail across that meadow to those cows."

Betty made one more try.

"Pan," she said, "take Shag with you this morning to haze for you in case that stallion gets out of hand."

But Betty was talking to a stone wall.

"Shag's got lots to do without riding herd on me," Pan said. He grinned widely at Betty, waved his arm and stepped out into the deep freeze.

A few minutes later Betty and Willie and Diana, looking out the window, saw Pan and Wang Leather appear out of the gray haze. The big black was snorting, and with his neck bowed plunged through the first of the drifts that ringed the field in front of the house. He was not bucking, and Betty could see the dynamic power of the animal as he gracefully plowed shoulder deep through the first drift—and then man and horse were gone, and Betty sighed, shook her head and returned to her bread dough.

The morning hours dragged slowly by for her. She went about her various chores around the house, occasionally glancing through the windows out towards the wild windswept opening. She, Shag, Willie and Diana ate lunch an hour late. There was little talk around the table.

The children turned in for their afternoon nap and Shag headed for the barn. Another hour went by. Betty looked at the clock, turned on the radio and sat down in the homemade rocking chair staring intently into the dying storm.

At two-thirty Betty felt a mounting panic: it would be dark in two hours. And then Shag crashed through the front door, his eyebrows and vague chin whiskers matted white with frost. A cloud of blue steam rushed with him through the open door.

There was a wild look in the boy's eyes as he stood there, his legs wide apart. Betty jumped to her feet.

Shag yelled, "Wang Leather's back. Back at the barn. Wang Leather's back with his saddle on, Pan's saddle. It's pounded all to hell!"

They learned much later what had happened. Out on the wide opening, over a mile from the ranch buildings, Pan was confronted with several high drifts of snow that ran like ridges across the meadow. They all ran in one direction. The troughs between them were swept almost clean of snow. Visibility was much more open now and Pan looked back along the snow ridges trying to see how far they went.

Unfortunately Pan had forgotten about the heavy-jawed wolf traps that he had strapped to his saddle horn before leaving the corrals.

Wang Leather was impatient. He fought his head and began to dance and then crowhop.

I'll take a chance, thought Pan. We'll hit the drifts straight on and hard—come out on the lanes between them.

Wang Leather plunged into the first drift, floundered, got his feet under him and sprang high and hard through the far part of the drift onto the lane.

Man, oh man, thought Pan. This fellow's sure got what it takes.

Now they were into the second drift. With a mighty plunge Wang Leather broke through into the second lane.

One more, thought Pan, and we've got her beat.

Now they were plunging and rearing through the third drift. Pan felt one of the traps touch his knee. He glanced down. The saddle strings had been cut in two with the drift plunging, and the heavy traps hanging over the saddle horn were swinging loose. This was dynamite.

"Easy, Wang old boy—easy."

Pan pulled up hard on his hackamore bit but he was too late. They were out on the third lane. The big stallion swung down the opening between the drifts. The bunch of traps slapped the horse across the shoulder. This was all he needed.

With a wild squeal the black downed his head and broke in two. Pan gripped his powerful leg muscles into the horse's body, dug his spur rowels into the stallion's belly, pulled up hard on his reins and leaned back in the saddle.

There was a swishing sound as the great animal hit the ground with terrific force and the traps swinging in a wide arc smashed Pan across the stomach. The impact was so terrific that blood spurted out of Pan's nose and his ears. Blackness seemed to be closing in on him as the stallion hit the ground again, and then once more came the traps, flying at his mid-section with frightful speed. Pan could hear distant thunder and the world seemed to stand on end in a crimson haze.

My feet, he thought. I've got to get clear of the stirrups. He'll drag me to death.

And then his feet were clear and Pan was going over the back of the horse. He saw the hind feet snapping through the air, the whole outline of the hoofs, the coronets, the fine black hair of the fetlocks, coming at him out of red fog—and then a brilliant white flash against the sky.

Gnawing dreams, strange figures were dragging at him now. They were trying to tell him something— something about waking up—something about freezing to death. It was like fighting his way out of a nightmare for when Pan opened his eyes he saw the pool of blood about him and gagged on the red froth that threatened to suffocate him.

He tried to rise to a sitting position, heard a strange click and the lights went out again.

Pan came to. He didn't feel the cold but the outside edges of the pool of blood around him had frozen.

Something's broke bad, he thought. Must be my backbone. I'm crazy—crazy as a loon. Never should have packed those traps. What's going to happen now to me and those folks back at the ranch?

The wind had stopped. The sky was a pale icy blue. Dusk had come—night and darkness and silence were descending. Pan couldn't feel the gnawing cold that was creeping into his body, nor did he feel any pain from his injuries—but he knew only too well that time was running out on him, and there was nothing in the world that he could do about it—just lie there helplessly—freezing slowly but surely to death. Maybe there was an hour left him, maybe two hours, and then it would be all over.

But Pan hadn't counted on the lightning decisions and the resourcefulness of his wife Betty and the kid Shag.

Pan heard the rattle of harness first—then Shag's loud command.

"Steady there, Nigger, easy, boy."

Then Pan heard Betty call to Shag.

"I'll break through this drift on Wang Leather's tracks ahead of Nigger."

And then they were there in the lane with him, Betty and Shag, and saddle horses and old Nigger, the work horse, with his harness on, pulling a crude Indian-style pole travois.

For a moment Pan heard the gasps and shocked exclamations as Betty and Shag came suddenly upon the mess that he was—but only for a moment. Then strong arms were lashing him down on the travois. Darkness took charge of him again—and then there was the heavenly warmth of the ranchhouse, the strong smell of coffee and the happy voices of children about him.

There was a long confused nightmarish period during which time Pan has a few recollections. He vaguely remembers Shag and Betty placing steaming hot towels over his stomach, Betty's reassuring smile. He was in the living room on the wide-poled, hay-filled bunk used as a day couch, for he could see a string of windows across the front of the room.

He remembers the darkened windows, then through them the light of day. The monotonous sound of the gas lamp, a dull buzzing noise, told his subconscious mind that another night had come, and with it his mind dragged back to life and he was wide awake, conscious of the terrible pains in his hips and the searing knifelike stabs that ran through his stomach. Betty rested her hand on his forehead.

"You've a fever, Pan," she said. "Shag's going to try to ride around the Algak Mountains for help in the morning. If he can make it to Christensons', he'll phone for a plane and a doctor."

Now began the gravest part of Pan's ordeal. His stomach was distended with blood. He blacked out every time he tried to rise to a sitting position. The pain in his back and hips was almost unbearable.

He hadn't the slightest idea of the extent of his injuries, but he was sure of one thing—that he was going to die.

He thought with horror of the complications that Betty and the children would be faced with if he died in the house while Shag was away. No matter how fast a ride Shag made, it would be several days before either Shag, a plane, or anyone else would be able to break back through to the ranch—and then of course there was always the chance that Shag wouldn't make it through to Christensons'.

The vague light of a new day spread through the room as Pan made his decision. Since his case was hopeless, it was better that Shag stay here to keep the house in wood and water, feed the cattle, shoot a beef for meat when the family ran out of food. This way Betty and the kids and Shag would survive the winter. It was the only sure way that they would come through. So Pan turned on his vast will power to keep Shag off the trail and Betty convinced that he was healing—but the pains never ceased.

Every evening Pan would hold a ranch meeting. He was educating Shag and Willie in the tricky lore of cattle-raising. Shag made his daily report on the cattle, describing each animal, its habits, its distinctive personality differences from its fellows. Shag soon knew each cow from the other, and could describe them to Pan's satisfaction.

Betty would play soft music on the radio, and the strange homey noises and voices from an outside world, far removed from the realities of their own grave plight, would give them all cheer and hope—all but Pan. He thought of all the things that he had not yet accomplished and now would never do.

On the tenth day after his injury a particularly bad spasm took hold of him—the worst he had yet experienced. He thought of the bottle of brandy that was cached in the house and asked Betty to bring it to him. He hadn't dared to touch it before, for fear it would weaken his will and he might reveal his conviction that he was going to die.

But now everything was under control. Great piles of wood were racked up under the eaves of the house, the cattle were making it in good shape, and Betty and Shag and the kids were organized. Now if he could just numb the pain for a few minutes. The brandy might do it.

Betty found the bottle. She propped Pan up a little with a hay-filled pillow and deposited the bottle, a glass and a pitcher of water beside the bed.

"I'll drink her down straight," Pan said.

Betty walked to the radio and turned it on. Pan took a long gulp from the bottle, gagged for a moment, then reached for the water glass.

"Wow," he exclaimed. "Not used to the stuff. We'll try it again."

Betty stood by the bed watching him. Pan took another long swig from the bottle. This time he didn't gag.

"Have a drink on the house," said Pan. "One for old time's sake."

"No thanks, Pan. I don't need it. But I think you've had just about enough."

Pan was raising the bottle again. His pain was leaving him. He felt a warm glow creeping over his mind and his body.

"I'm going on my own private little drunk—right now—and all by myself."

He gurgled the bottle almost to the halfway mark.

"Wowie, wowie, woman, don't take this brainwasher away from me. I'm going to town."

Pan carefully set the bottle down on the table beside the bed.

"I want to get a few points straightened out in my mind," he said.

Now for the first time in ten anguished days and ten fitful, nightmarish nights, Pan was partially freed of pain.

It was then that the truth suddenly flashed upon him like northern lights across the sky. He might live. The realization was so startling that it took several minutes to sink in.

"How long have I been here?" Pan asked Betty.

She told him. He mulled it over. If he had lived for this long, then the crisis between life and death must have passed. He might live on now unless some complication set in, but there was little doubt in his mind that without medical aid he would be a hopeless cripple.

Shag pushed through the door. He looked with surprise at Pan and the half-empty brandy bottle.

"Come over here, Shag," said Pan. "How's the weather outside?"

"Warmed up some, about thirty below now."

"The snow?" asked Pan.

"Settled a lot in the last few days."

"O.K., boy, do you figure you can get around the mountains to Anahim Lake?"

"On Wang Leather I can," he said, a determined gleam in his eyes. "And I can ride him, too. I've ridden him around the corral twice and he never bucked with me. Wang Leather can make it," Shag repeated, "maybe thirty-five hours' riding—maybe forty—I don't know. But I've been thinking about it every day."

Pan knew Shag had been raised around horses and even at fifteen years of age was a bronc rider of no mean ability. He also felt sure that once the stallion got clear of the first drifts on the big opening he would settle down to a hard, ground-gaining walk.

"Go to it, boy," Pan said quietly. "Get Andy Christenson to stay with the phone until he lines up a plane. Figure out how long it will take you to ride back here from Anahim, add one day to that, and tell the outfit we'll have a big green-tree-smoke smudge going out on the lake three miles from here.

"If Andy can't line up a plane up north, tell him to phone Russ Baker in Vancouver and explain what's happened. Russ is head of Central B.C. Airways now— he'll organize it even if he has to fly in himself."

Shag gulped down his lunch and at one o'clock that afternoon Betty, standing at a living room window, called out a blow-by-blow description of Shag's progress with Wang Leather.

"He's coming out of the gate real fast, but Shag's holding him in. Not bucking. Through the first drift. They're in front of the house now. My, they hit that next drift hard. Shag's riding him just as smooth as an old bronc twister. They're going into that patch of timber over by the creek. Now they're out of sight. Hurray— hurray for Shag."

"Good boy," said Pan. "Good boy, Shag, good girl, Betty."

Then with a long sigh Pan slumped back on the bunk and dropped off into the deep sleep that he needed so badly.

Shag's ride that February in 1948 was a phenomenal feat of endurance, grit and horsemanship. The narrow Indian trail which in some places was not marked, in others nonexistent, was a hard one to follow. Wide detours had to be made around impassable drifts. Snow was swept off frozen lakes leaving treacherous glare ice.

He broke through into the dark pine forests of the Algak foothills long after nightfall. Only a top woodsman

could have followed the snow-drifted trail to this point.
Now ahead of him reached the long winter's night and
the black jungles and frozen muskegs of Ulgatcho
Indian land. It would take even greater woodsmanship
and luck to see him on the beam through the long hours
to daylight.

Occasionally he pulled Wang Leather to a stop to
let him get his wind. The deathlike silence about man
and horse seemed to close in and almost suffocate him.
The horse's loud breathing, the creak of saddle leather,
the hoofs crunching through the snow, were the only
sounds to break the silence of the northern night.

Once Shag heard a far-off wail. Then a strange
mournful dirge rose higher and higher to reach its zenith
and drift slowly off into the silence of the lonely snow-
bound land. Wang Leather heard the wolves too. He
snorted and plowed with even more zip into the deep
snow ahead. Branches and snags reached out at Shag from
the blackness, scratched and crashed against his moosehide jacket and chaps. His face was scratched and bruised
and bleeding.

Above the treetops Shag could see the Milky Way and
the vast star-studded heavens blinking and twinkling.
Sometimes they seemed to be right on top of him, and
then an eternity away. Gradually stars changed, shifted
positions as the night wore on.

Shag looked often over his shoulder to keep tabs on
the North Star, for in case he swung off the trail, he
knew he could still keep his direction by heading a few
degrees west of due south. He would be able to cut back
to the trail when daylight broke.

Dawn finally came. It was a dull gray lifeless light that crept steadily into the forests. Dark objects began to take on shape and form. Wang Leather was plowing through deep snow along the edge of a vast opening to the west.

"It can't be!" exclaimed Shag. "It can't be the Algak muskeg. We could never have come this far in this deep snow."

But when he swung in his saddle, looking back over his shoulder, the sight almost took his breath away. Towering thousands of feet above him in almost sheer walls, rose the white spires and peaks of the Algak range.

Shag had made a record ride under the worst conditions, and by far the toughest part of the long trail now lay behind him. He was over forty-five miles from the Home Ranch. He still had nearly thirty to go. But soon he would reach Andy Holte's turnoff and the trail from there to Andy Christenson's at Anahim Lake would be well used, hard packed and the traveling fast.

At exactly one P.M. by Andy Christenson's time, Wang Leather walked stiff-leggedly into the Christenson yard. He was white with lather. He was leg-weary. He was scratched and scarred, but by the proud way he held his head, by the bow in his neck, and by his unfaltering stride, anyone could see he was not windbroken or heartbroken. He was as sound as ever.

This was really a miracle ride. Now the Home Ranch lay seventy-five miles around the Algak range, forty-five of those miles in belly-deep snow over seldom-traveled country. Only twenty-four hours had elapsed since Shag had crawled Wang Leather's frame and ridden away. Any man who can bring a horse through that sort of mileage in good condition deserves a heap of credit. And Shag was only fifteen.

Upon Shag's arrival, the Christenson ranch burst into action, and the long, complicated telephone relay began station-to-station, from the far outpost of Anahim, through Kleena Kleene, Alexis Creek, Williams Lake, Ashcroft to Vancouver, and then far north again to Prince George where it was arranged that, if flying weather held on, a plane would land on the lake, three miles from the Home ranchhouse, three days hence.

As usual, Andy and Dorothy Christenson came through in this crisis to help their distant neighbors. Andy loaned Shag a fresh horse to relieve Wang Leather on the long journey home, and insisted that Shag's older brother, Jack Thompson, who was working for Andy at the time, accompany Shag back to the Home Ranch.

"It will be a big help and relief to both Pan and Betty to have an extra man back there while Pan's out in hospital," Andy Christenson said.

The first plane attempt to pick up Pan didn't turn out so well. Something went wrong with the motor and the pilot crash-landed a few miles beyond Quesnel. The pilot escaped without injury, but it took another three days before Russ Baker in Vancouver was able to line up a second plane flight into the headwaters of the Blackwater River.

On February 13, sixteen days after he had his crack-up with Wang Leather, Pan was lifted into the plane on the snowbound lake, and that evening stretchered into the Quesnel hospital.

Dr. Gerald Ramsey Baker had plenty of experience.

His many fabulous trips to save trappers' and ranchers' lives are part of the history of the North Country.

Dr. Baker didn't go in for preliminaries.

"The first thing we're going to do with you," he said to Pan, "is to x-ray you from your toenails to the top of that thick skull of yours. Then we'll know where we stand."

"Whatever you say, Doc," Pan said.

When the doctor walked into Pan's room the next day with a nurse and the x-rays, he gave no inkling of his feelings, but as soon as he stepped through the door, Pan could sense that all was not too well and that Dr. Baker was prepared to do some heavy explaining.

"Not too bad, Pan," said the doctor with that informal way of talking he had. "You took a beating, boy, but you'll be all right when we get through with you. You just have to follow orders, that's all."

The x-rays of Pan's hips showed that his pelvis was split an inch and a quarter apart. While this looked formidable, Dr. Baker explained that after six or nine months in hospital, Pan would be able to walk again. He reassured the Top Hand that, if all went well, it was even possible that some day, when the muscles that were torn away from his hips had mended, and the pelvis closed, he would be able to ride a gentle horse.

The doctor and a small crew went to work on a traction outfit, rigging up pulleys, stretchers, ropes and weights. Pan's legs were stretched out at strange angles and weighted down, until they coincided with a very businesslike-looking blueprint. The rigging was complicated, but when it was properly adjusted it gave Pan a considerable feeling of relief. Within a week Pan was able to rise to a sitting position without passing out. Dr. Baker was delighted.

Pan studied the mechanism and the theory of this system of pulleys, springs and weights. At the end of his second week in the Quesnel hospital, and a few days before he was to be flown to Vancouver for his final long treatment, Pan dropped a bombshell in Dr. Baker's lap.

"I've done some thinking, Doc," Pan said. "And I've plumb made up my mind to one thing—and that's for sure. I'm going to get Tom Corless to fly me back to the Home Ranch just as soon as you can rig me up with a set of harness like this and a blueprint of how to tangle me up in it."

"Whoa there," broke in Dr. Baker. "Whoa there, Pan. Hold on a minute. Back there—more than two hundred miles from the nearest hospital—you wouldn't have a chance if anything went wrong with you. There's a chance the bone specialists in Vancouver will have to perform an operation—your hip muscles are pulled clean away from the bone and are going to take some working over. If you go back there into the jungles at this stage in the game you're ruining your life. You'll never ride again. You'll be lucky if you can walk."

But Pan had made up his mind. He looked at Dr. Baker.

"Betty and the kids are back there on the Blackwater. There's a herd of top whiteface cows, a hundred and forty head of horses, sixty of 'em brood mares in foal. No tellin' what could go wrong. The outfit needs me, Doc, so I'm flyin' back there. There's no use to argue. Rig me up a blueprint of how I've got to be stretched out. We'll work from there."

When I finally got out to Vanderhoof I picked up a letter Pan had written me the day before bush pilot Tom Corless flew him back to the Home Ranch. As usual he was brief and his letter contained very little information. Just said that he had got messed up with a bronc but was headed back to the Home Ranch.

I called Dr. Baker at Quesnel. I can still remember the last words the grand old doctor barked at me over the phone.

"You never can tell about Pan. Miracles have happened, you know. That tough, bullheaded son of a gun may fool us all. Some day we might see old Wild Horse Panhandle come once again pancaking it across the Fraser bridge on the back of a cayuse—but I don't know."

CHAPTER XVIII

To Ride Again

AND THEN THE SPRING FLOODS washed across the interior of British Columbia. Again creeks became rivers, valleys filled with water. Lakes took the place of green meadows and grass. Reports of atomic fallout on watersheds in B.C. drifted in to us. We were warned not to drink surface waters from streams.

Ranchers cursed and raved and shook their fists at the belching sky. People in cities and towns scurried into their offices and houses, remarking on what extraordinary weather we were experiencing, but we who lived outdoors noticed a strange sinister light in the sky. There was no color—just a pale whitish gray. Boats replaced the wagon, the tractor, the saddle horse.

But at Rimrock this flood was only a token of the frightful flood of the year before. At least there were patches of land sticking above the water, and it was possible to reach cattle stranded on islands. Many cows were separated from their bawling calves.

Rhino was a great swimming horse. I wore shorts and a raincoat and swam sackfuls of oats out to marooned cows and yearlings.

The floods started in April. A weird soggy sun gleamed

dully from a pale white incandescent sky. Bugs of every
description—mosquitoes, black flies, botflies, deer flies,
bulldog flies, heel flies—rose up out of the boggy land in
great hungry clouds to torture all living creatures.

Along towards the middle of May we received some
definite news about the Phillips family. What Gloria and
I were told was extremely disquieting.

Tommy Walker, once the head guide of South
Tweedsmuir Park, and his pack train had only recently
slugged through the Home Ranch country en route to
Vanderhoof. He reported to us that the country around
the headwaters of the Blackwater was submerged under
a vast blanket of mud and slush. The grass was watery,
the range poor. Some of Pan's cattle had died, and he had
lost a great many horses because of the deep snow and
several layers of heavy ice crust.

Pan's physical condition had improved, but early one
morning Shag had reported to the house that he and his
brother, Jack Thompson, were unable to help Pan's pet
Thoroughbred mare give birth to her first colt.

"Turn me out of this bunch of snares," Pan had commanded the boys. "And move fast. Get a pail of hot water
and the Lysol. We ain't gonna lose that mare and colt."

The boys carried Pan across the opening to the feedyard. One of them ran back for the water and the dis-
infectant. Pan crawled painfully up to the fast-weakening
mare. He disinfected his hands. His exploratory exam-
ination revealed that the foal's head was twisted back and
one foot was bent under.

Pan had had much experience delivering calves and
colts. It takes a lot of strength and know-how to readjust

the unborn animal into the proper position for delivery. Pan was successful in delivering the colt, but the strain was terrific and he keeled over on his face when it was all over and the mare and colt were safe.

When Tommy Walker saw the Top Hand it was some three weeks after the mare and colt episode, and he found Pan paying a heavy price for the strain he had inflicted on his back and leg muscles. His hips ached day and night, he slept fitfully and never seemed to be rested. He looked like a sunken-eyed, living skeleton. Betty was worried and distraught.

Tommy Walker told me the Thompson boys were leaving for Anahim the fifteenth of June, and Pan was planning on starting on the long-unused wagon trail to Quesnel on the same day to pick up the many supplies needed for the months ahead and for haying. Betty would drive the team with Pan and Diana in the wagon, and Willie would ride behind on a saddle horse. If all went well, there were no breakdowns, and not too many hundreds of fallen trees across the road, which of course Betty would have to axe or saw out, the family would make it to Quesnel in two weeks' time.

Pan's message to me was to meet him at the Traveler's Rest in Quesnel no later than July 5.

I thought of Pan and Betty and the swamps and muskegs they would have to navigate on the wagon road to Quesnel. East of the deserted Indian village of Kluskus, 160 miles from Quesnel, there were wide stretches of swamp where there was no regular trail, and if you were unfortunate enough to be on the trail in a wet year in late spring or early summer, you had to use a long pole, jabbing it into the soft oozing sod to pick out a safe way through the mess. If you misjudged just once, and then tried to drive your team through, you could very easily lose the whole outfit in the bottomless bog. The remains of wagons and bits of harness were still to be seen here and there on the edges of the mud-bottomed creeks of that area a few years ago.

Indians of the Kluskus area were smart enough to avoid these bottomless pitfalls by getting completely out of that part of the country before the frost had gone out of the ground. The Indian migration to Quesnel usually took place early in June, and the vast swamp country was left to its own spooky transformations until August, when the ground tightened up. Then the few Indians that lived beyond the swamp area would return to their log hovels on their saddle horses and in their Bennett buggies, broke of course after their summer in town, but happy indeed to be able to negotiate the barriers and reach home.

On July 5 Gloria and I saddled up and rode the thirty-five miles from Rimrock into Vanderhoof to check on the Panhandle expedition. I put a call through to Dr. Baker and was told that the Phillips family had not arrived in town.

On July 15 we again rode to Vanderhoof and I put another call in to the doctor. He was as worried this time as were both Gloria and I. He told me that every member of the five Indian clans between Nazko and the Home Ranch had arrived in town at least two weeks before, and from all intelligence he had been able to gather, the country through the back swamps, due to the extremely wet year, was absolutely impassable.

The time element at this stage of the game was most important. Betty and Pan and the kids could easily have been stuck somewhere along the trail for the past three weeks—quite possibly without food. Some fast thinking and some quick action were needed.

Ken Silver from Vanderhoof drove me to Quesnel and then on over the back-bush road to Art Lavington's cattle ranch at Nazko, where I picked up two saddle horses and a pack horse and struck into the swamp country in search of Panhandle's outfit.

When I rode through the last outpost of civilization, the Nazko Indian village, two old Indians, one of them Chief Morris, an old friend of mine from Batnuni days, told me that they had been informed by moccasin telegraph that Bert Smith, who now owned the Batnuni Ranch, and Slim Dolvin, his top cowhand, were driving a pack train through to Anahim Lake. They planned to go through the Home Ranch en route and check up on Pan.

This was very good news. Smith would ride into the Home Ranch before I could. But if Pan and his family had already left the ranch for Quesnel, and were stuck in the Lashaway swamps, Smith would miss them completely.

Now I decided to ride day and night using the old tried and true method of covering a lot of country without killing off or breaking the hearts of willing horses. Four hours' ride; two hours' feed, water and rest. Four hours' ride again, two hours off.

My ride was uneventful and uninteresting. The rain turned on again the first night on the trail and I never quite dried out the rest of the trip. I reached the swamps on the third night out of the Lavington ranch, and spent the following two days cutting and laying decking across impassable mudholes. My horses got a good rest. There were no tracks of the Home Ranch wagon.

Many hours after dark the following night I slugged through the last of the mud to the deserted Kluskus Indian village and the open side-hill country. An hour before daylight I unpacked and hobbled the horses on a little meadow near the last safe crossing on the flood-ravaged banks of the Blackwater River. The big question was whether Bert Smith's pack train had made the Kluskus crossing, and at daylight I found the answer in the shod horse tracks imbedded deep in the mud. The tracks were between two and three days old. Bert had beaten me to the Home Ranch and by now he would know what had happened to the Phillips family.

I realized that there was nothing that I could do at the Home Ranch that Bert Smith and his man couldn't do. In case Pan was seriously ill, my best bet would be to send in a plane, to bring him out if necessary. I reined my saddle horse around and led the others down our back trail. Five days later I made town and got in contact with bush pilot Tom Corless.

Besides himself, Corless' tiny plane had a load capacity of no more than two hundred pounds of man or of supplies. We sent in the essentials in food. Corless was back at Quesnel by nightfall the following day with the news that Pan and his family had never left the ranch and were coming through the constant series of emergencies in good shape. The Thompson boys had made it to Anahim in June, and Shag had returned with a pack-horse load of flour, rice, macaroni and coffee, enough to tide the family through the long wet period.

Since that time Betty had shot and butchered a moose, herded the cattle and horses onto the summer range—

and Pan had made himself a crude set of crutches. The Top Hand was still using the traction a good deal of the time, and had become a fairly good baby-sitter. It had been arranged that Bert Smith would drop off another pack-horse load of food on his return trip through the Home Ranch.

The Phillips family's long-postponed expedition to Quesnel was slated to arrive in town between the first and fifth of September.

As I waited at the Fraser River bridge at Quesnel for the wagon to arrive on that September day in 1948, I watched the fancy new cars and trailers rolling along the highway, looked at the neat modern houses and flower gardens across the street, the well-fed townspeople scurrying along to the restaurants for their mid-morning coffee break to split up their well-ordered, eight-hour day. I reflected on the contrast between the lives of the average modern-day, security-minded, luxury-soaked citizens of our country—and those other folks who were still slugging it out on our last frontier.

Particularly I thought of Betty. How could the average woman of our day and age even conceive of her grueling nine-month ordeal—the never-ending, day-by-day, month-by-month emergency, not knowing whether her husband would live or die, whether she and her children would themselves survive.

I thought of Betty's terrifying loneliness; of her slithering on her hands and knees through the dismal birch to bring down an ugly-headed monster of a moose, of her quartering up, hoisting and lashing down the bloody meat onto the backs of unwilling pack horses. Of her driving their herd of cattle out of the mud and water many miles up into the awesome, grizzly-infested Itcha Mountains to put them on the dry summer range.

I thought of Betty running down, outbluffing and catching, then haltering and throwing the heavy harnesses on the big team of horses—and finally—the two hundred long back-breaking miles she had to drive the wagon through the swamps and mountains, axing and sawing out great crisscrossed piles of down timber that blocked the trail, to get her crippled husband and children out to civilization.

It would be hard for even the horsiest, most range-minded women from our Western ranches to believe that any woman would be physically and mentally able to accomplish what Betty had during that winter and spring and summer of 1948.

Betty was smiling as the wagon clattered over the bridge and drew up alongside of us.

"Where's Pan?" we yelled.

"He's hiding," Betty called over her shoulder. "See you all later."

Art Lavington and I jumped on the back of the wagon box and pulled ourselves up and over the high end gate. And there he was—that tough old Pan—lying there on his straw tick, looking half ashamed.

"Don't let on you see me, boys. Let's get through this mob."

Dr. Baker was amazed by Pan's great improvement, but he still thought that Pan should go to Vancouver for treatment. Although the new x-rays showed that the split in the Top Hand's pelvis had pulled together somewhat, and his hip muscles were mending, still Pan was running the risk of being permanently crippled.

We all told Pan that it was sheer madness to return to the Home Ranch—that he could never make it physically or financially by returning. We urged him to close down his isolated layout, sell what cattle and horses he had left and move into Quesnel, or up with Gloria and me onto Rimrock Ranch or River Ranch in the Nechako Valley. What good would a crippled rancher who couldn't afford even one hired man be, back there in the jungle? we argued.

But Pan's mind had not been idle those long months he had been on his back. He had made his plans, and now he would carry them out. As usual, nothing could swerve him from his decision, and, in character, he made light of what lay before them.

"Nothin' to it, boys," Pan drawled to a bunch of us who had gathered in his ground-floor, two-room suite at the Traveler's Rest.

"Everything's going to be easy. All we got to do is get back there to those swamps and get to work."

And so Pan and Betty and Willie and Diana, and the big team, Nigger and Doc, and Willie's buckskin pony and Diana's little collie dog rolled out of town a few days after the gang of us broke up and headed back to our own ranches and our own problems, problems that now seemed very small.

It was on this homeward journey that Betty had her terrifying experience with the grizzly bears. The Phillips family had been on the trail for ten days. They had four miles to go to reach the ranchhouse. It was late afternoon and growing bitterly cold.

"Do you want to dangle on home and get the fires lit, Betty?" Pan suggested. "It'll warm up the house before we bring Diana in. Those horses you're drivin' are home now, you can just forget 'em."

"Good idea," Betty said. "See you in an hour."

Betty touched Alec in the ribs with her boot heels and the old cow horse left the wagon at a lope.

The ranchhouse had been closed down now for more than six weeks.

Betty was trail worn, and she was cold. The thought of the big warm ranchhouse made her amble right along. She finally reined up Alec at the barn which stood some two hundred yards from the house on the edge of the timber.

Old Alec was nervous. He snorted several times, threw his head and tail in the air, pulled back on his bridle reins. Betty thought he was acting strangely. It was not in character.

She tied the cow horse up in the barn, threw him a forkful of hay, and stepped through the barn door.

The grove of tall spruce trees reached up high above the undergrowth on Betty's left side. On her right the open meadow stretched away into the distance.

A feeling of uneasiness gripped her as she walked tiredly towards the ranchhouse. She thought she heard growling sounds and strange crunching noises coming from the ranchhouse yard.

Suddenly, not thirty feet in front of Betty, the willow bushes parted and the bald head of a grizzly stuck out, and then his shoulders. He surveyed the opening, sniffed into the air, swung about, and his moldy-looking dark brown rump swung into view as he crashed back into the bush.

Betty wanted to scream. She swung about facing the barn she had just left.

I'll dash back there quick, she thought, but her decision was cut short. Not fifty feet behind her another, smaller grizzly broke out of the brush and without looking in her direction, started shuffling towards the barn.

"My God," Betty breathed. "I can't go back. I must reach the ranchhouse. I can't get panicky."

She angled out further on the meadow away from the heavy undergrowth as she quickened her stride. She remembered Pan's words: "Don't run fast away from a grizzly." The house was now closer. Another bush shook and swayed off to her left. A heavy body crashed through the brittle dry sticks.

I've almost made it, Betty thought. Only a hundred feet to go.

A four-foot-high picket fence fronted the long ranchhouse. Betty reached the gate. She was breathing hard. She looked over the picket fence, then she stifled a scream. Her knees started to give way beneath her. The remains of a dead horse were strewn about the lawn in front of the porch. Two huge brown forms, grizzlies, hunched up half asleep on the porch.

Four other bears were tearing, biting and pulling away at the scatterings of the dead horse. She stood within fifty feet of this gruesome scene. Suddenly Betty's mind cleared. A horrifying thought broke through her mounting panic.

Her crippled husband—the children—the wagon.

My God, if Pan isn't warned he will drive up to the house, the team will run away, and Pan's rifle is under his bedroll out of reach! I've got to reach that wagon. They're not far away now. I'll have to walk by these grizzlies. Maybe with the good Lord's help, I can make it.

Betty told me that the first hundred yards or so that she staggered off up the meadow towards the wagon road seemed like the longest mileage she had ever walked in her life.

She saw another bear swinging slowly along towards the ranchhouse on the edge of the road. She moved off the old wagon tracks towards the open meadow. This grizzly, the eighth one she had seen, went on by, not paying the slightest attention to her, and finally in the distance Betty's ears caught the faraway whine and pound of the wagon.

The horses were moving in on the trot. Betty does not clearly remember meeting the wagon or Pan's answer to her shouted warnings. But Pan grins when he drawls out the finale of Betty's grizzly ordeal.

"Well sir, I just got a good hold of that old 30.06. I pulled out my six-shooter, the .44—and we drove up to the house. I told Betty to hold the lines with a death grip.

"Some of those grizzlies wouldn't leave that dead cayuse. So, well, I just had to bear down on four of 'em. Killed the four of 'em before we could get into the house. I guess Betty and Willie thought a war had broke loose when I started popping those caps. There was twelve grizzlies all told in the group that had taken charge of the Home Ranch."

Pan always swung his arms around over his head when he finished telling the story.

"I sure didn't want to kill those four grizzlies, they were just cleanin' up the carcass of old Blackie who had died there in the yard.

"But hell, we couldn't get into the house, and I didn't

want to hang around there in the cold all evening trying to scare those old boars away."

A year later I saw Pan and Betty on their next trip to town. I arrived in Quesnel the day after Pan had distinguished himself at the annual cattleman's hoedown. In a far corner of the huge lumber barn, where a bar had been set up and drinks were being passed out freely, Pan, surrounded by a group of his cronies, leaned on his crutches, sucking and biting away at a cigar while he watched the dancers, among whom Betty was a popular partner.

Suddenly, to everyone's astonishment, Pan hobbled to the door, snorted loudly, and with a mighty heave threw his crutches out into the dark.

"Those toggles have had it," yelled Pan. He whirled around, stalked out onto the dance floor, tapped Betty's partner on the shoulder and danced off with her.

Once again Pan proved up on one of his outlandish brags. He never used the crutches again.

The Phillips family made a big comeback. Pan always went on the principle of making the most of what you've got. Hit your problems from every angle. Try anything if it makes sense—you're never licked unless you think you are. He had a kind of Pollyanna attitude that he had been putting successfully to work.

He opened up an Indian store on the Home Ranch. He turned the old bunkhouse into an all-Indian home quarters where Indians could stay overnight. The Top Hand started a commission system with the Blackwater Indian Alexis family who were live wires and were anxious to get to live like white men.

Peter Alexis and his hunchback brother George had good contacts with the great tribe of Indian trappers, the Ulgatchos, who lived west of the Home Ranch towards the coast. Most of these bush Indians did their trading at Bella Coola. Their fur catches were quite fabulous. Traders had gone all out for years to establish themselves with these super trappers to get a chance at their fur. A season's catch sometimes amounted to thousands of dollars for a single family.

Pan traded food, dry goods and various other articles to the Indians for beaver, mink, muskrat, marten and fisher pelts. He contracted his freight with the Alexis boys.

The Top Hand did so well with his store and his trading that he was able to put Shag back on his payroll and clean up his debts. His herds of cattle and horses had been steadily increasing while he was convalescing.

The following year Pan started riding a sidesaddle. In the fall of 1951 he discarded it for his old stock saddle, and then in 1952 I heard over the radio and read in a number of Canadian and United States periodicals about the rancher in central British Columbia who with his wife and two children had arrived in Quesnel with their beef herd after more than three weeks on the trail.

Of course, the commentators who made the announcements over the radio, and the reporters who wrote up the event, had no idea of the background behind their story. They were merely reporting the news that a rancher named Panhandle Phillips and his family had just completed the longest toughest beef drive on the North American continent.

CHAPTER XIX

The End of the Party

ON OCTOBER 17, 1952, some time after Pan's much-publicized beef drive, a great new event took place in the lives of Gloria and myself.

At the immaculate new St. John Hospital perched high on a wooded hill overlooking the village of Vanderhoof and the clear green waters of the wide Nechako River, Pat Patterson, the blacksmith, had joined me in a marathon walk back and forth, up and down the second-floor hallway of the hospital. Pat's second wife, Frances Maynard, a friend of Gloria's from Vancouver, was resting comfortably in a room in the maternity ward near the delivery room where Gloria had disappeared hours before.

"What's the deal?" I asked Pat. "I brought Gloria up here at five this morning—now it's twelve o'clock, and still silence from that room down there."

"Nothing to it," Pat said. "My first family—four kids—it was always like this."

The door to the delivery room opened up and a smiling sister of Charity appeared followed by a tall nurse carrying a bundle. The two were headed in our direction. I stiffened in my tracks.

"Take it easy now," Pat snapped at me.

"It's a girl, Mr. Hobson," said the sister. "Congratulations. She is the image of her father."

The nurse opened up the bundle very carefully.

"I'll be damned," I gasped. "Look, Pat—a full head of hair already—and she's smiling instead of howling."

"How is Gloria?" Pat asked. "If the father is in such a trance I'll have to ask the question myself."

"She's just fine," said the nurse. "You can see her in just a little while now."

Tall, clean-cut young Dr. Ed McDonnell walked out of the ward in his long white and green uniform, removing his gauze mask as he approached us.

"Congratulations," Ed said, slapping me on the back.

Now stocky-built, cheery-faced Dr. Alvin Mooney, head surgeon of St. John Hospital, walked briskly down the hall from Frances' room. Pat looked panicky.

"How is she?" he blurted.

"Not for a while yet." Dr. Mooney smiled. "But it won't be long now."

Dr. Ed McDonnell turned to Dr. Al Mooney.

"There's one empty room down the hall. I think we better have these men put under sedation at once. Neither of them is standing up at all well under the strain."

My daughter was named Cathy. Pat's boy, born a short time later, was named Mike.

Several days after Cathy had arrived in our midst and I had returned to my duties at Rimrock Ranch, two large cattle trucks roared up the hill to the hospital and parked in front of the steps. Four weather-beaten, high-booted cattlemen crawled out of the drivers' cabs and milled about for several moments collecting armfuls of packages, then started stiff-legged up the steps to the hospital door.

Panhandle Phillips packed a slight limp as he shuffled ahead of the others carrying two long rectangular boxes. Behind Pan, easily recognizable by his rugged face, rocklike jaw, and his extraordinary choice of hats, this time a dusty, bloodstained Homburg sitting squarely in the middle of his head, gingerly stepped Lester Dorsey, the horseman contractor of the Home Ranch who had built and driven the famous horse harrow.

Walking beside Lester was a trim-built, mild-acting man who resembled, in almost every respect including the keen twinkle of his sea-blue eyes, the great Will Rogers. This was Andy Holte, the fabulous teamster who was described in my book *Grass Beyond the Mountains*.

Behind him, a husky, blue-eyed, blond young man wearing perfectly fitting cowboy garb gave Andy a shove.

"Hurry up, Dad," he bellowed. "Is this the first stairs you ever crawled up?"

The powerful young cowboy was Tommy Holte, a top bronc rider of British Columbia, Andy's son, who pioneered with Pan and myself the building of the Home Ranch on the Blackwater back in 1935.

The four ranchers were a long way from home. After some confusion the men maneuvered their bulks through the door of Room 217 where Gloria was sitting up in bed reading.

Tremendous greetings, welcomings and excited exclamations went the rounds. Suddenly a crescendo of grunts, wails and bawlings of bulls floated up through the window into the hospital room.

"Sounds like range bulls out there," exclaimed Gloria. "Are you boys bringing them up to pay a call on me?"

"Just a bunch of old bulls we've brought all the way from the Home Ranch and Anahim to trade to Rich for some of his Lionheart bull calves," Andy explained.

While Gloria asked questions of the cowmen whom she hadn't seen for many many moons, Pan and Lester began undoing the various packages. Several new books, masses of pale pink carnations and long-stemmed red roses, a bottle of Drambuie for Gloria's private consumption and several bottles of Mumm's champagne.

Gloria was overwhelmed.

"My goodness," she exclaimed. "I always knew you boys could do almost anything in the woods, in the mountains and on the swamps—anything from bringing your cattle and horses through and saving your friends against amazing odds—building log houses and barns, fences and roads, accomplishing the impossible—but I just never thought you would be able to track down roses and carnations and the best of champagne anywhere in this North Country."

"Us boys know our way around." Pan beamed. "Was in Anahim when the wire from Rich about the new little cowgirl arrived. These other boys here was just getting organized to bring their beat-up old bulls to Rimrock to trade, so I just loaded my bulls too and jumped in with 'em.

"Rich said in his wire to me we ought to see the new little heiress. Said she was born with a full head of hair with bangs made to order. Can't understand it—Rich bein' so bald and all."

Now Pan barked. "Open up the champagne, Lester. Can't you see there's a lady sufferin' for a relaxer for her nerves—and there you are—standin' there like an idiot."

The following day when the men drove their trucks of bulls into the ranch yard at Rimrock they told me that there had been quite a reunion in Gloria's hospital room.

"Hardly enough room to stand up in there," Pan said. "Maynard Kerr and his wife came in, George Hobson from his Little Creek Ranch, Pat Patterson, all dressed up in his formal clothes, Bob Reid and Sam Cocker. Now with me as one of the leaders, little Cathy has got a whole herd of godfathers.

"I'm tellin' you, friend—those brides of ours sure topped out our outfits for us. When we built that first shack back there on the Blackwater and was livin' on moose meat and beans, we never thought we'd end up with two of the best cattle ranches in the country, women who can take the bush in their stride, and each of us with little cowgirls who'll be breakin' out our broncs for us in a couple of years."